Evangelism God's Way

Manual

Discipleship, Educating, and Leadership

Go ye!
Matthew 28: 19-20

Every Christian is called and commissioned to make disciples of all nations, to evangelize all those they come in contact with...

Deborah Nembhard-Colquhoun

Evangelism God's Way
Manual

Discipleship, Education, and Leadership

Deborah Nembhard-Colquhoun

General Editor: Carrie L. Jeffrey

Copyright © 2011 Deborah Nembhard-Colquhoun

All rights reserved. No part of this book may be used or reproduced by any means, graphic, electronic, or mechanical, including photocopying, recording, taping or by any information storage retrieval system without the written permission of the publisher except in the case of brief quotations embodied in critical articles and reviews.

Unless otherwise indicated, all Scripture quotations are from the Holy Bible King James Version ©. Used by permission.

Evangelism resource information at the end of the manual are offered as resources. These resources are not intended in any way to be or imply an endorsement on the part of Evangelism God's Way, nor can we vouch for their accuracy.

All funding resources for non-profit organization are from CharityVillage.com© website. Used by permission.

Witnessing to Mormons-Key Elements are from http://www.frontierner.net/-bcmmin. Used by permission, John Farkas.

All questionnaire forms are from Tomevangelisumunlimited.org. Used by permission.

Articles, Quick Tips: Witnessing to a Jehovah's Witness and Religion vs. Christianity: What's the difference and The "Jesus" of the Cults are from www.Jude3.com. Used by permission, Jason Carlson and Ron Carlson.

WestBow Press books may be ordered through booksellers or by contacting:

WestBow Press
A Division of Thomas Nelson
1663 Liberty Drive
Bloomington, IN 47403
www.westbowpress.com
1-(866) 928-1240

Because of the dynamic nature of the Internet, any web addresses or links contained in this book may have changed since publication and may no longer be valid. The views expressed in this work are solely those of the author and do not necessarily reflect the views of the publisher, and the publisher hereby disclaims any responsibility for them.

Any people depicted in stock imagery provided by Thinkstock are models, and such images are being used for illustrative purposes only.

Certain stock imagery © Thinkstock.

ISBN: 978-1-4497-1812-1 (sc)
ISBN: 978-1-4497-1870-1 (hc)
ISBN: 978-1-4497-1811-4 (e)

Library of Congress Control Number: 2011930220

Printed in the United States of America

WestBow Press rev. date: 6/8/2011

Evangelism Analysis/ Research among Churches in Canada

Most Church growth is a result of recruiting members from other congregations (this is not growth).

According to statistics, in actuality Church growth is reported to be at a rate of 2%.

The Church (the body of Christ) is at ease in Zion.

Most Churches (the body of Christ) have no idea that all believers are called to evangelize.

Some believers are interested in starting an evangelism ministry but have no idea where to start.

The Church (the body of Christ) has lost its zeal to witness for Christ and its fervent love for others.

There are no evangelism strategies in place for outreach in most Churches.

Most Churches (the body of Christ) believe that it is the pastor's job to reach the unsaved.

A low percentage of the Church (the body of Christ) have some sort of evangelism going on but have no discipleship or follow up plan in place.

There is a great harvest that needs reaping.

The world is filled with opportunities for the message of the Gospel to be heard and received, but on a large scale the church is sinfully silent.

Contents

Introduction ix
1. Why Evangelize? Seventeen Points 1
2. What is Evangelism? 15
3. Evangelism Challenges & Encouraging Perspectives 17
4. The Office of the Evangelist vs. Evangelizing 22
5. The Power for Ministry 27
6. Evangelist in Revival 31
7. There is Power in Prayer 48
8. Prayer Evangelism 62
9. Proper Covering is Needed in Evangelizing 65
10. Do and Don'ts in Evangelism 70
11. Evangelism God's Way 72
12. Styles of Evangelism 77
13. Example Script 80
14. Event Evangelism 85
15. Door to Door Evangelism and Critics 87
16. Tract & Evangelism Tips 89
17. Your Witnessing Audience 91
18. Witnessing to Cults 94
19. Creation vs. Evolution 119
20. Bible Doctrines in a Nutshell 123
21. Choosing an Individual for Ministry 132

22. An Argument for Christianity 136
23. Law and Grace................................. 138
24. Will Christ Come Again?......................... 140
25. Life in Three Tenses............................. 141
26. In the Twinkling of an Eye........................ 142
27. The Duty of Self-Testing 143
28. Challenges to Holy Living........................ 145
29. Seven Distinguishing Marks of a Christian 146
30. Sample Follow-up Plan 147
31. Sample Follow-up Script and Letters 149
32. Teaching Outline for Baby Christians 155
33. Characteristics to Finish Well...................... 161
34. Christian Joy 163
35. God's Missionary Call 165
36. Anticipating a Great Harvest 167
37. The Holy Spirit's Work in a Community 169
38. Evangelist Covering the Earth 171
39. Evangelism Leaders Responsibilities: A & B........... 173
40. Sample Ministry Plan 176
41. Sample Evangelism Forms & Schedules............... 185
42. Sample Evangelism Questioner 190
43. Where to Get Free Evangelism Materials and Resources.... 195
44. How to Obtain Ministerial Credentials 202
45. Funding Resources for Non-profit Organizations......... 206
46. Obtaining Charity Number........................ 217
47. Mission Opportunities—Links 222

Special Acknowledgements: 223
Bibliography.. 225

Introduction

With God in the centre of any evangelism project, we are confident that with the right attitude, much commitment, encouragement, and accurate training and resources, the body of Christ can increase immensely its effectiveness in reaching people who have not accepted Jesus Christ as their Lord and Saviour. The enormity of the task of evangelism may lead one to discouragement. To help diminish some of the negative factors and provide adequate tools for the task, we have prepared this manual, which outlines information that will boost the effectiveness of evangelism efforts and increase the opportunities for winning souls. We decided, in part, to put this manual together because we have experienced great difficulty in finding complete resources all in one place within the city of Toronto for facilitating an evangelism ministry. If you decide to pursue the ministry of evangelism, you won't have to go through the same experiences we have encountered. This informative manual is useful in all aspects of evangelism: teaching, training, witnessing, follow up, discipleship, starting your own evangelism ministry, and many other tasks.

1

Why Evangelize?
Seventeen Points

1. **Mankind separated himself from God and as a result is spiritually dead and physically depraved.**

   - Romans 3:23 states, "For all have sinned and come short of the glory of God." God did not originally create mankind to be separated from him. This separation caused mankind to be spiritually dead, physical depraved, and destined to die, Romans 5:12.

   How did this separation happen?
   - In Genesis 2:17, God told Adam that in the day he would eat of the forbidden fruit, he would "surely die." This death refers both to spiritual death (Gen. 3:8) and to physical death. Thus, mankind was spiritually dead at the original fall; however, physical death did not occur right away. When we are born again, spiritual death is rendered null and void. Physically, however, "And as it is appointed unto men once to die, but after this the judgment" (Heb. 9:27). According to Paul in Ephesians 4:18, "Having the understanding darkened, being alienated from the life of God through the ignorance that is in them, because of the blindness of their heart." Mankind can only be alive again spiritually if he accepts Christ as his Lord and Saviour. Colossians 2:13 says, "And you, being dead in your sins and the uncircumcision of your flesh, hath he quickened together with him, having forgiven you all trespasses." This Gospel needs to be preached to all mankind.

   - Mankind does not have the ability or the desire in himself to reconnect to God, to overcome sin and death, or to bring himself from the state of spiritual death back to life. Only the supernatural

Sovereign God can. God knew mankind's incapability and this is why He sent Jesus Christ and also provides the Gospel to draw mankind back to Himself. We must understand that salvation is God's work and that He redeems us as a part of His work. God made reconnection and new life possible at Calvary, but such life needs to come to fulfillment in us. God works continually within us by rejuvenating our hearts. It is our duty now to provide the Gospel so the work He has started will be established.

2. **Jesus came to earth and died to redeem mankind back unto Himself.**

   - "For God so loved the world, that he gave his only begotten Son, that whosoever believeth in him should not perish, but have everlasting life" (John 3:16).

   - God does not want anyone going to hell. 2 Peter 3:9 states, "The Lord is… not willing that any should perish, but that all should come to repentance." One can truly come to repentance only through the Gospel. The Scriptures indicate that the way people come to be saved is through evangelization. They come to salvation by hearing the Good News of Christ and then believing.

   - Romans 8:1–4 states, "There is therefore now no condemnation to them which are in Christ Jesus, who walk not after the flesh, but after the Spirit. For the law of the Spirit of life in Christ Jesus hath made me free from the law of sin and death. For what the law could not do, in that it was weak through the flesh, God sending his own Son in the likeness of sinful flesh, and for sin, condemned sin in the flesh: That the righteousness of the law might be fulfilled in us, who walk not after the flesh, but after the Spirit."

   - The apostle writes, "And you, being dead in your sins and the uncircumcision of your flesh, hath he quickened together with him, having forgiven you all trespasses" (Col. 2:13).

3. **Evangelism is the responsibility of all Christians. It is not an option, but a command. God gave us the Gospel to share.**

   - Have you ever wondered why, after an individual is saved, God does not take him or her up to heaven immediately? I have…I have even thought about the point that Christ is still preparing a place for mankind. But the ultimate truth of the matter is that we are here on earth for only one thing and that is to preach the Gospel. God can speed up His construction in heaven any time, but He chooses not to because He has imprinted upon mankind His plan to use us as His vessels for carrying redemption to the world.

- Christ commands all Christians in Matthew 28:19, 20, saying, "Go ye therefore, and teach all nations, baptizing them in the name of the Father, and the Son, and of the Holy Ghost: Teaching them to observe all things whatsoever I have commanded you: and, lo, I am with you always, even unto the end of the world."

- Paul writes in 1 Corinthians 9:16–23, "For though I preach the gospel, I have nothing to glory of: for necessity is laid upon me; yea, woe is unto me, if I preach not the gospel! For if I do this thing willingly, I have a reward: but if against my will, a dispensation of the gospel is committed unto me. What is my reward then? Verily that, when I preach the gospel, I may make the gospel of Christ without charge, that I abuse not my power in the gospel. For though I be free from all men, yet have I made myself servant unto all, that I might gain the more. And unto the Jews I became as a Jew, that I might gain the Jews; to them that are under the law, as under the law, that I might gain them that are under the law; To them that are without law, as without law, (being not without law to God, but under the law to Christ,) that I might gain them that are without law. To the weak became I as weak, that I might gain the weak: I am made all things to all men, that I might by all means save some. And this I do for the gospel's sake, that I might be partaker thereof with you."

- "Preaching the Gospel," according to Dr. Rondo Thomas, Vice President of Canada Christian College, "is not only by words but also by lifestyle."[1] Our lives are open books that the unsaved may read. What are they to read when they look at us and the lives we lead? They should see Christ in us and all over us; they should read the story of Christ-like character in us. What would Christ do? We are to exhibit the same character as Christ would. In this way, people may read the living words in the Bible as they are being applied to our lives. For example, our lives can show the fruit of the Spirit, which are, love, joy, peace, longsuffering,

---

1   Dr. Rondo Thomas, Vice President at Canada Christian College

gentleness, goodness, faith, meekness, and temperance (Galatians 5:22-23).

- It is impossible for the sovereign Christ to be alive in us and for His presence to go unnoticed.

4. **God compels us to practice Evangelism.**

    - If you are under compulsion to do something and you refuse, don't you expect some repercussions? 1 Corinthians 9:16 says, "For though I preach the gospel, I have nothing to glory of: for necessity is laid upon me; yea, woe is unto me, if I preach not the gospel!" We are not our own, we belong to Jesus. Yes! You might say we were given free will and don't have to be puppets. Please don't forget that Satan was also given free will, but he chose the wrong path, and as a result lost his position for eternity. Think about that! Disobedience is sin.

5. **We evangelize to promote congregational growth.**

    - No one likes to go out to evangelize and feel intimidated by the prospect. Let's face the truth, however, that no one will come to your congregation unless you go out. If you just sit there, pray, and believe you are going to have a full church, then think again; it won't happen. Faith without works is dead. Over the last two thousand years, growth in the church has been directly related to the church going out into the world to evangelize. Jesus had His disciples go out and He expects us to go out, too. The church in the Acts of the Apostles grew because Christians went out. Even throughout this past century, churches in our society grew because their members went out to evangelize.

6. **There is a great harvest of souls in the world to reap**

    - Matthew 9:37b, 38, says, "The harvest truly is plenteous, but the labourers are few; Pray ye therefore the Lord of the harvest, that he will send forth labourers into his harvest." The world is the field where the ready harvest is, the Word is the seed in the unsaved hearts (the ready harvest) and the workers are the Christians.

- God has used others to plant seeds and others to water. He has even done the conviction and is now looking for those that are available to reap the ready harvest. Are you a ready vessel, available to be used for Christ in winning souls? If you are, all you need to do is take up your baskets, go to the field and God will fill them with souls.

7. **How will they believe unless they have heard?**

    - Romans 10: 14-17, 14 "How then shall they call on him in whom they have not believed? and how shall they believe in him of whom they have not heard? and how shall they hear without a preacher? And how shall they preach, except they be sent? as it is written, How beautiful are the feet of them that preach the gospel of peace, and bring glad tidings of good things! But they have not all obeyed the gospel. For Isaiah said, Lord, who hath believed our report? So then faith cometh by hearing, and hearing by the word of God."

8. **Everyone has not heard the Gospel.**

    - We so often overlook our city and our neighbor when we assume that they have heard the Gospel. We are so wrong. Did you know that, even in a civilized city such as Toronto, Canada, there are still many people who have not heard the Gospel? After going door to door in this very city of Toronto, we discovered that not everyone has heard the Gospel. When asked, "Do you know Jesus Christ?" their reply was "Who is that?" Don't think that they are being sarcastic. How do you know if they are telling the truth and what evidence do you have? After we introduced Jesus Christ to them, we could detect their sincerity. They showed interest, and, to top it off, the eyes that shed tears, revealed the truth that they knew nothing about Christ. One of the reasons why they knew nothing about Christ is due to the many different cultures that have immigrated to Canada. These immigrants apparently had not been introduced to the Gospel in their previous country of residence. Also, because of their other religious and cultish practices, they would not have had anything to do with Christianity.

    - The preaching of the Gospel is very limited on television programs and radio stations in Canada as well as some other parts of the world. The few programs that exist are often not watched or listened to because the Gospel is foolishness to unsaved people who would rather watch and listen to ungodly things. In other parts of the world, the TV and radio stations may be effective in reaching the lost, but here in Canada it is only reaching one percent according to studies conducted by "Evangelism God's Way" team. Most of the listening audience of Christian television and radio are Christians. Most programs are not designed to reach the lost, but are for Christians to sow their financial seeds into. How sad! How I pray for a media blast of the true Gospel that will not only get the believers' attention, but also attract unbelievers who happen to click on such a channel! Some unbelievers also reported that they are turned off from watching the Christian channels because they do not see the real Gospel being preached in most cases.

- Not only is the Gospel foreign to some immigrants, but it is also foreign to many citizens that have been born in Canada. This is because a very large percentage of households do not expose their children to Christianity. Christ is banned from most public schools as many people prefer darkness rather than the things of God, who is Light. Sadly, most parents are more concerned that their children receive a good education, and participate in recreational activities, and leave no time to expose them to the things that will nurture their souls. Most children will grow up to adopt satanic lifestyles, embrace worldly values, and accept secular philosophies.

- Also, many unbelievers are not seeing the Gospel because many Christians do not exhibit the Word of God in their lives. Unbelievers who do not read the Word are left with only darkness to see. It is time that Christians get serious and stop being encumbered with the yoke of sin and start allowing their lives to be free of darkness so that the light can be seen.

- Regardless of those who do not want to hear, all will eventually hear. Matthew 24:14 says, "And this gospel of the kingdom shall be preached in all the whole world for a witness unto all nations; and then shall the end come."

- God is doing a new thing in these last days because His coming is at hand. Like the church in Sardis (Rev. 3:4), God is raising up individuals who refuse to let their garments be defiled and who WILL allow the light of God to shine through them.

9. There is a real hell

- As believers, I don't believe we are conscious of the fact that there is a real hell and that soon this reality will be revealed. Matthew 13:49 - 50 states, "So shall it be at the end of the world: the angels shall come forth, and sever the wicked from among the just, And shall cast them into the furnace of fire: there shall be wailing and gnashing of teeth." Will you wish at that time that you did more evangelizing? "Too late!" might be your cry. There will be no more chances for unbelievers, including your love ones. Let us put away the things that have us so preoccupied - that which will soon pass away - and occupy ourselves with those things which have great eternal value (evangelism).

- **Matthew 7:13:** "Enter ye in at the straight gate: for wide is the gate, and broad is the way, that leadeth to destruction, and many there be which go in thereat."

- **2 Thess. 1:7-10:** "And to you who are troubled rest with us, when the Lord Jesus shall be revealed from heaven with his mighty angels, In flaming fire taking vengeance on them that know not God, and that obey not the gospel of our Lord Jesus Christ: Who shall be punished with everlasting destruction from the presence of the Lord, and from the glory of his power; when he shall come to be glorified in his saints, and to be admired in all them that believe (because our testimony among you was believed) in that day."

- **Rev. 20:15:** "And whosoever was not found written in the book of life was cast into the lake of fire."

- Hell is real. The book of Luke describes the eternal destiny of a rich man who died and went to hell. While in hell he called out to Abraham to have mercy on him, and asked if he could send Lazarus (a poor man who was a diseased beggar, who also died, but went to heaven) over to hell so that he could dip the tip of his finger into some water to cool his tongue, for he was being tormented in the flames of hell.

10. It is the duty of a Christian to love.

- One of the commandments is "Thou shalt love the Lord thy God with all thy heart, and with all thy soul, and with all thy mind. This is the first and great commandment. And the second is like unto it, Thou shalt love thy neighbor as thyself. On these two commandments hang all the law and the prophets." (Matthew 22:37-40).

- Some may profess that they love God but are not obeying His commands. To disobey His commands results in watching our neighbor go to hell. This is not love. 1 John 4:20 says, "If a man say, I love God, and hateth his brother, he is a liar: for he that loveth not his brother whom he hath seen, how can he love God whom he hath not seen?"

- If we refuse to evangelize, we are disobeying the Lord. The Scripture also says, "Not every one that saith unto me, Lord, Lord, shall enter into the kingdom of heaven; but he that *doeth the will* of my Father which is in heaven" (Matthew 7:21 italics mine).

11. Thousands of people are dying every day without hope.

There is an epidemic of disease. People are dying because of many different factors. Whether the medical system has failed, or through diseases which have no cure, it is appointed unto every man once to die. All men *WILL* die sooer or later because of sin. The true Gospel is mighty enough to provide them with eternal hope. After death, there is no more opportunity for salvation.

12. We are in the last days before Christ's Return.

No one knows the time of Christ's second return. However, all believers should know the season because Jesus told us what to look for.

- Luke 12:54-56, "When ye see a cloud rise out of the west, straightway ye say, There cometh a shower; and so it is. And when ye see the south wind blow, ye say, There will be heat; and it cometh to pass. Ye hypocrites, ye can discern the face of the sky and of the earth; but how is it that ye do not discern this time."

- Matthew 24:32-34,"Now learn a parable of the fig tree; When his branch is yet tender, and putteth forth leaves, ye know that summer is nigh: So likewise ye, when ye shall see all these things, know that it is near, even at the doors. Verily I say unto you, This generation shall not pass, till all these things be fulfilled."

- 2 Timothy 3:1-7, "This know also, that in the last days perilous times shall come. For men shall be lovers of their own selves, covetous, boasters, proud, blasphemers, disobedient to parents, unthankful, unholy, Without natural affection, trucebreakers, false accusers, incontinent, fierce, despisers of those that are good, Traitors, heady, high-minded, lovers of pleasures more than lovers of God; Having a form of godliness, but denying the power thereof: from such turn away. For of this sort are they which creep into houses, and lead captive silly women laden with sins, led away with divers lusts, Ever learning, and never able to come to the knowledge of the truth."

- Within the church we see the signs of the time. I Timothy 4:1-3; "Now the Spirit speaketh expressly, that in the latter times some shall depart from the faith, giving heed to seducing spirits, and doctrines of devils; Speaking lies in hypocrisy; having their conscience seared with a hot iron; Forbidding to marry, and commanding to abstain from meats, which God hath created to be received with thanksgiving of them which believe and know the truth."

- Jesus also said that the last days are going to be like the days of Sodom and Gomorra. These days are even worse than the days of Sodom and Gomorra. All these things have been fulfilled. Jesus said that when these things start to come to pass, we should look up for our redemption draws nigh.

- Believers have many road signs indicating when Jesus will return. We have been traveling since the book of Genesis, gone past many fulfilled exits, and now we are approaching the last exit of Revelation. We have discovered from our road map (the Scriptures) that the final exit is just up the road. We have enough indicators. We have been approaching the last exit for awhile now (the last days) and we are paused at the last exit too long. The only sign left for us to read is the rapture or destruction.

13. We are anointed to preach the Gospel

- Luke 4:18 "The Spirit of the Lord is upon me, because he hath anointed me to preach the gospel to the poor; he hath sent me to heal the brokenhearted, to preach deliverance to the captives, and recovering of sight to the blind, to set at liberty them that are bruised."
- Let us preach the life-changing Gospel. We preach not by might, nor by power, but by the Spirit of the living God.

14. People are being offered false substitutes…

- There are so many different cults that have risen up, especially in these last days. Unfortunately, people are joining them because they are searching for a solution for life's troubles, for the emptiness they feel inside, and the need to be reconnected to their true maker (God). People are so vulnerable and it is our responsibility to provide them with help (the Gospel).

15. Jesus Christ himself was an evangelist.

- He "preached the Gospel" (Luke 20:1). One of the reasons He did so was as an example for us. Let us follow in His example.

16. Evangelism is the spirit of the church.

- In the same way that the human body is dead without the spirit, so is the church dead without evangelism. The church can only move from a dead state to a living state if it evangelizes. We can also compare a church that is not growing to being a dwarf. According to the North America English dictionary, a dwarf is "somebody of small stature due to medical reasons, usually somebody with an average-sized body but unusually short limbs, or somebody with growth hormone deficiency." Let's equate the words "dead" or "dwarf" to the church. Doesn't something seem wrong with this picture? Yet we continue to be nourished Sunday after Sunday, not to mention Bible study nights, and revival services as well as our own personal spiritual feeding time at home (with the Word). Are we the only ones that are being nourished while others are perishing? In this view, it appears as if the food is only going to a couple of limbs. How spiritually obese are some Christians! It is good that we cannot develop Gospel problems from over-consumption of the Word of God. What about the other **malnourished** limbs that should be fed from the universal church?

17. When we share the Gospel, we are providing people not only with eternal benefits but also with temporal benefits.

- The hope of eternity can never be comprehended by the finite mind. According to Scriptures, heaven can only be described as breath taking. Oh! The splendors of heaven will never cease! In heaven, gold is the most insignificant thing because it is the asphalt on the streets. We can't even imagine what our dwelling will be like. It must be magnificent since Jesus is there preparing it for us. This new eternal destination will be much better than the original Garden of Eden that we have been locked out of as a result of our sin. Heaven will be mind-blowing: we will just pass out and get up speechless, not even able to believe our eyes. When we gaze upon God, all we will be able to do is cry, "Holy! Holy! Holy! Lord God Almighty." Do you know that there will be no need of light there because God will be our eternal light? There we will no longer be servants, but kings and queens. We will have the privilege of being served by angels. When the angels approach us, they will hide their faces saying, "Holy! Holy! Holy!" Why? Who are we? It has not yet been revealed what we will be but... *we will be like Him*. Do you know that believers are the bride of Christ? There will be no sickness, no pain, no sadness, no sorrow, and absolutely no form of sin in heaven. The old things will all have passed away, and behold, all things will become new. That day is soon approaching and we need to work the work of Him who called us before it is too late. There is no evangelism in heaven.

- What about now? Our future eternal destiny is not the only life that is wrapped up in Christ. Many of the situations that we presently face in life have their solution also wrapped up in Christ...the Word. People nation-wide are in despair because of natural causes as the forces of darkness are working hard. Principalities and powers and rulers of darkness in high places have set up their camp everywhere and are fighting against us. If one is in Christ, he is protected from all harm..." The angel of the LORD encampeth round about them that fear him, and delivereth them" (Psalm 34:7).

- Psalm 91 says, "He that dwelleth in the secret place of the most High shall abide under the shadow of the Almighty. I will say of the LORD, He is my refuge and my fortress: my God; in him will I trust. Surely he shall deliver thee from the snare of the fowler, and from the noisome pestilence. He shall cover thee with his feathers, and under his wings shalt thou trust: his truth shall be thy shield and buckler. Thou shalt not be afraid for the terror by night; nor for the arrow that flieth by day; Nor for the pestilence that walketh in darkness; nor for the destruction that wasteth at noonday. A thousand shall fall at thy side, and ten thousand at thy right hand; but it shall not come nigh thee. Only with thine eyes shalt thou behold and see the reward of the wicked. Because thou hast made the LORD, which is my refuge, even the most High, thy habitation; There shall no evil befall thee, neither shall any plague come nigh thy dwelling. For he shall give his angels charge over thee, to keep thee in all thy ways. They shall bear thee up in their hands, lest thou dash thy foot against a stone. Thou shalt tread upon the lion and adder: the young lion and the dragon shalt thou trample under feet. Because he hath set his love upon me, therefore will I deliver him: I will set him on high, because he hath known my name. He shall call upon me, and I will answer him: I will be with him in trouble; I will deliver him, and honour him. With long life will I satisfy him, and shew him my salvation."

- "I have been young, and now am old; yet have I not seen the righteous forsaken, nor his seed begging bread " (Psalm 37:25).

- Romans **1: 15 says,** "For I am not ashamed of the gospel of Christ: for it is *the power of God unto salvation* to every one that believeth; to the Jew first, and also to the Greek." (italics mine). Let us highlight the sentence that says, *'the power of God unto salvation.'* What an assurance! The stain of sin does not have to keep people in bondage because God is powerful enough to free all men from sin.

Lets us look further into the believer's blessing in Christ

God is the source of all our blessing, in the heavens and on the earth. . The believer's entire blessing is found in Christ. Ephesians 1:3 says, "Blessed be the God and Father of our Lord Jesus Christ, who hath blessed us with all spiritual blessings in heavenly places in Christ."

Ephesians 1:3 tells us that all our blessing is locked up in Christ. Therefore, we need to be in Christ in order to receive all our blessings. The Holy Spirit works to apply the Gospel to our lives and then comes to dwell within us. Once we are in Christ, there are no limits to the blessings of God. It is way beyond our comprehension; it stretches across the entire world and reaches to the heights of heaven and even beyond. Therefore, we need to live by the Spirit, stay away from sin and open our eyes to see what we are entitled to as believers. It is not about what others say, but what God says. In His Will (the Bible) we can find all of our inheritance. There are treasures untold: treasures of authority, power, love, faith, grace and mercy....

Matthew 5:45 declares that God's blessing falls on the just and on the unjust, but only those who are in Jesus Christ are given the blessings of the heavenly places. We are also entitled to receive temporal blessing. However, the focus is not on earthly blessings because it doesn't matter what we receive on earth as it will eventually perish. Spiritual blessings will last forever. No matter how much earthly blessing we acquire on earth, if we do not have spiritual blessings, we cannot be really satisfied, and in the end, we have no peace. This is why there is still a void no matter how much wealth and fame we accumulate here on earth. When we receive our spiritual blessing, we become complete in Christ. We experience peace, joy and happiness that passes all human understanding. 1 Peter 1:24 says "For all flesh is as grass, and all the glory of man as the flower of grass. The grass withereth, and the flower thereof falleth away." Spiritual blessing is everlasting.

Although we have sinned and come short of the glory of God, our blessing still stands. Once we come into the fold of faith through believing in Christ, we are entitled to all the blessing that God has in place for us. God will not go back on His promises. Before the foundation of the earth, His plan was put in place to bless all believers. Among the many blessings listed in Scriptures, here are a few: Although we are undeserving, God's grace was given to us freely. (2 Timothy 1:9). Our redemption is in Christ: (Romans 3:24; Ephesians 1:7; Colossians 1:14). Thus, the forgiveness of our sins is in Christ: (Ephesians 1:7; Colossians 1:14). In Christ we will be resurrected: (1 Corinthians

15:22). In Christ we have obtained an inheritance: (Ephesians 1:11). In Christ are hidden all the treasures of wisdom and knowledge: (Colossians 2:3). We can do all things through the Lord: (Philippians 4:13). Christ is in us as He indwells us by His Holy Spirit: (Romans 8:9-11; Colossians 1:27).

Conclusion

Once we accept Christ and walk in the perfect will of God the blessing of the Lord will manifest itself in our lives. Also, we will not only be blessed while we are on earth but also after death when we reach eternity.

2

WHAT IS EVANGELISM?

At its most basic, evangelism presents Christ through the power of the Holy Spirit in spreading the good news of the Gospel to the world. The result of evangelism is that mankind will turn from their sin and accept Jesus Christ as Lord and Saviour of their life

Evangelism happens when believers deliver the message of the Gospel in cooperation with the Holy Spirit. Without the work of the Holy Spirit, the message is of no effect. It is the Holy Spirit who anoints the word and causes the unsaved to be convicted of their sin. Evangelism is all about the *agape* love of God - God's perfect love extending to humanity. This awesome love has been extended to all believers; therefore, evangelism is a divine privilege. When we exhibit this divine love to the unsaved, a divine spark will reach their heart and cause them to be saved from eternal damnation.

The message of evangelism should always remain the same; the unsaved need to be aware of their sinful condition, Christ came to save; they need to repent and accept Jesus Christ as their Lord and Saviour. They also need to know that if they choose to reject the gift of salvation, the consequence will be hell.

Evangelism takes three forms:[2]

a) Evangelize by preaching the Good News about Christ to the world. This can take the form of a sermon or even a personal testimony.
b) Evangelize by being an example of Christ's transforming love, which can be observed by the world.
c) Evangelize by providing finances/resources to other believers who are called to preach the Gospel in other parts of the world. This is

---
[2] www.oocities.org/mattperman/union.html

how we can be fellow workers in the harvest. One might not able to speak but can aid others in sowing the seed.

How should we really preach?

- *By our lifestyle-* Others should be able to look at us and identify that we are Christians without us telling them.
- *With confidence and authority-* This will add power to your preaching, and it will reveal the sovereign God. People will have no choice but to recognize that there is a divine Being behind such authority.
- *Like Paul-* With perseverance (Colossians 1:21-23)! Preaching can come with many trials and testing, so preach like Paul who endured through numerous hardships until the end.
- *Not for gain-* Preach the Gospel; not for personal gain, but to exalt Jesus Christ.
- *In the Holy Spirit-* With full dependence upon the Holy Spirit. Without the Holy Spirit, people will only see and hear flesh speaking.
- *With "wisdom of words"* (1 Cor. 1:17). It is important to "Study to shew thyself approved unto God, a workman that needeth not to be ashamed, rightly dividing the word of truth" (2 Timothy 2:15).
- *Only preach the true Gospel* (Gal. 1:8). Only the true Gospel can cause true change. Substituting the true Gospel with any other gospel won't do it!
- *The truth about mankind* (Romans 10:3). Mankind is spiritually dead and is in need of a Saviour.
- *About Christ, salvation, hell and heaven.*
- *With love, sincerity and goodwill.*
- *Be "blameless and harmless" and "shine as lights in the world"* (Philippians 2:15).
- *Preach with warning.*

3

Evangelism Challenges & Encouraging Perspectives

Like any other ministry, evangelism can be very challenging…Some people start out very enthusiastic in evangelism and after a few months or even years, have become discouraged to the point of complete withdrawal. To endure, it is very important that we understand certain perspectives.

The idea of entering into an evangelism ministry can be very exciting. For many people, this is a dream come true. They will shout, "Let the excitement begin!" They see souls from every corner of the earth coming to Christ, with workers connecting to them, and the heavenly host coming down to assist them. Oh yes, that can happen, but unfortunately it is not often the case. Looking from the outside in can be very deceiving because there are many challenges within the walls.

Challenges:

No immediate results

Many cults

Political, demographic, social and economic differences

Different ethnicities

Afraid of the unknown

Lack of time

Being alone

Lack of passion or unmotivated

The Gospel must be presented reflecting both the positive and negative consequences

People are more interested in spirituality and worldly pleasure rather than Christianity

Criticism, rejection or ridicule

Undignified job

No financial gain

Challenges vs. Encouraging Perspectives

It can be very discouraging when we put forth much effort to win the unsaved but see no results. If we understand the process of soul winning, we would be very happy to do what we can and leave the results in the hands of God. The evangelism process is multi-faceted. It includes: planting, watering, fertilizing, weeding and harvesting. We all play a part in the process, but the final results are up to God. Section one of this manual explained the soul-winning process in more detail. We may not experience someone coming to Christ through our evangelism efforts. However, each step of the process is very important and the bottom line is that God is being glorified in each step.

In every country we find different ethnic groups. Most ethnic groups have barriers of different religious backgrounds, wrong beliefs, and many dialects/languages. There can be many challenges in evangelism to these groups, but this is all part of God's plan. Jesus told us to go and witness to all nations which include different ethnicities. All are God's children and need to be saved.

Demographically, there are still many limitations due to political rules. However, there are great opportunities for entering many of the countries that have been closed to the Gospel for years. For example, Eastern Europe and the former Soviet Union have opened their doors to visitors. Christians can go in, still with restrictions, but they can find creative ways to share the Gospel.

Strongholds of Secularism have taken over the minds of many non-Christians and Christians alike. In secularism, we find that God is completely removed from human life. People live their daily lives without any fear of God or the need for God. Their lives are lived with little opportunity to receive the Gospel. Despite such challenges, God is still in control and will make a way so that the Gospel can reach them.

Evangelism can be very scary, especially when we are new in ministry. The fear of the unknown will discourage us, but we need to remember that we are not going into ministry on our own. God has called us and He will establish His ministry sooner or later. All we have to do is be faithful in our small beginnings and God will remain faithful. Our thoughts are not His thoughts, neither are our ways His ways. God is always in control.

Lack of time will limit the work of God from going on. We are so passionate to do God's work but lack the time to do it because of the cares of life and the society that we live in has us tied down. This is so wrong! How can we serve two masters? Yes, we are living in a different dispensation but we need to know our limits. We need to place God as our top priority and He will allow everything else to fall into place.

God has called many people into ministry who are afraid to go forth, and even after going forth, they are in great fear wondering if anyone will turn up to help them. They may also fear that those who they have with them in ministry might leave. It is very important to understand who it is we are working for and realize that He will always send someone to lift up our hands in battle. God promises His people that He will never leave them nor forsake them.

It is natural to feel unmotivated at times, especially given the fact that we have an archenemy who is fighting against us every minute. In times like these we need to encourage ourselves in the Lord. Through it all we need to learn to trust in Jesus and depend upon His Word. Another important encouraging perspective for evangelism is perseverance and having a good understanding that God is at work in winning souls. The apostle Paul did not have it easy, but through it all he persevered until the end. He knew in whom he believed and also looked forward to the crown that awaited him in glory.

Why do we worry about who will be saved in our efforts of evangelism? Once we are prepared, God will open the doors. He told us to seek and we shall find; knock, and the doors will be opened to us. Also, Jesus said in His Word that those who are hungry and thirsty for righteousness will be filled. He will create the opportunity for a person to hear the Gospel so that they can be filled. He will also create an opportunity for those who are ready to spread the Gospel. This is a divine appointment. He is sovereign enough to open doors we would never dream that would be opened to us. When Jesus commissioned us to go, He assured us that He would be with us even until the end of the world. He also outlined our work description, gave us the message that we are to preach, and sent the Holy Spirit to aid us. This message is no ordinary message, but is a life changing message. The message that will break through any world-view, worldly attraction, any other spirit…

Preaching another gospel has become the 'norm' among Christians. People love convenient preaching; they love to be tickled with news about how rich they are going to be, how God is going to wipe away their problems, and the power that they will have. It is also convenient to preach that God wants to save His people. Yes, it is God's greatest desire, except that repentance is necessary first. The true Gospel must include the positive and the negative - God's love and God's wrath. The negative side of the true Gospel is how sinners are measured against God's law so that they can see their depravity and be informed about the consequences. Convenient messages target only the symptoms and not the root cause (sin), and are designed to please people, and cover their emotions, needs and problems. Despite its temporary gratification, this gospel is powerless to save. God will take care of the symptoms but His intention for the Gospel is to save those who are lost through the power of the Gospel. Evangelism is not sharing any other gospel, but is sharing the "Good News," which includes: Jesus died for our sins, we need to be saved, how to accept salvation and its benefits.

There is hardly any financial profit in evangelism. Many evangelists travel across the globe for years with only enough money to carry them to the next place. This could be because they received very little from their ministry, or, they received much but invested the money back into the lives of those who are in great need. Our motive in sharing the Gospel must be to please God and not be for our own gain. Otherwise, we are in for an unfortunate ride. Some are in full-time ministry for money. This will not go far in true evangelism. God often blesses His people financially, but not in all cases at all times. Sometimes He will allow us to be in lack, so that we can relate to people, and share our testimonies of God's goodness as we learn to rely only upon Him.

Rejection, criticism … will hinder us in our walk. Let us not get caught up in such a predicament by understanding that we will never please everyone. Facing rejection doesn't mean we fail. Yes, we might appear to be a failure in man's sight but not so in God's eyes. On the contrary, we are actually winners because we are being obedient to God's commission.

It doesn't matter what people think. What Christ says about our efforts is important. After all, it is God's work anyway! Therefore, the issue is not with us, but God. Hebrew 13:6 states, "So we say with confidence, the Lord is my helper; I will not be afraid..." In many situations we will find people who will criticize and reject us but it will not last forever. In order to continue on the road to success, we must put those encounters behind us and move on... our focus should be, "What next, Lord?" What can man really do to us anyhow? Yes, they can mock us, ridicule us, judge us and even kill our body, but only God can kill both body and soul. A very good motivational habit is to focus on what God thinks about us. Criticism will sometimes come for our learning. In this case, we must learn from criticism but make sure we don't dwell on it. We need to spit it out. In the future, let's focus on the positive and leave the negative behind. The negative comes from the enemy in order to rob us of what God truly wants us to achieve. These experiences are not new and we are not the only ones who have faced them. Jesus, the apostles, and mighty men and women in the Scripture faced them too. They did not allow criticism and discouragement to stop them but instead, persevered and overcame.

After going to seminary for many years and obtaining a degree in evangelism, the very thought of knocking on a few doors, and giving out a few tracts can be very humbling. What's the big deal? You might even grumble, "Can't anyone do that - like a little member?" Of course! However, you must remember that evangelism does not stop there. Evangelism is very broad and you should never despise small beginnings. As a matter of fact, it is very good to start from the beginning of a job rather than the middle or the end of it. Also, once God is in it He will bless it and take it to great dimensions. Let us not get caught up in being prideful. Let us work faithfully in whatever capacity God is calling us, with the right motives. Big starts don't always mean that God is in it. In our efforts, we must not get caught up in how or where we begin but in what we are doing for Christ and what He wants us to do. Let us minister in whatever capacity we can, and Christ will establish us. A knock at the door could be the start to the greatest revival on the planet, the start to a thousand souls being saved, and could even be the doorway to spiritual life for one who might be killed tomorrow in a car accident.

Despite the many challenges facing evangelism, we can still ignite the flame of revival over the entire nation. To do this we must embrace challenges in a positive way and go back to basics - evangelism God's way.

4

THE OFFICE OF THE EVANGELIST VS. EVANGELIZING

Let us look at three questions before we go any further
1. Who should preach the Gospel? (1 Peter 4:11; Eph 4:11)
2. How will a person know if they have the gift of evangelism? (1 Tim 4:5)
3. What is the difference between natural evangelistic ability and having a gift in preaching the Gospel?

Although the office and ministry of an evangelist is clearly stated in Scripture, it has become so misunderstood today in our churches and in society. A very clear and precise description of the evangelist's ministry can be found in Ephesians 4:11-16. "And he gave some, apostles; and some, prophets, and some, evangelists, and some, pastors and teachers, for the perfecting of the saints, for the work of the ministry, for the edifying of the body of Christ" (Ephesians 4:11-12). God knew what we would be facing in the world so He also provided us with power for ministry.

Notice that along with the apostles, prophets, pastors and teachers the evangelist's ministry accomplishes the same purpose: "For the perfecting of the saints, for the work of the ministry, for the edifying of the body of Christ" (vs. 12). It doesn't matter whether we are behind the pulpit or on the street: the ultimate purpose remains the same. This evangelist description does not fit all who call themselves evangelist. Many have occupied the office of an evangelist, but are not doing the work of an evangelist. One who is doing the work of the evangelist will be involved in three areas: *Perfecting the saints, doing the work of the ministry, and edifying the body of Christ.*

Let us look at what perfecting means: according to the English dictionary, it means "maturity," therefore, it is the spiritual maturing of the saints. This is the process of taking born again believers out of spiritual immaturity and bringing them into spiritual maturity. In such light, the evangelist MUST be Spirit-filled. Without the spirit of Christ, it is impossible for anyone to be perfected. It is not by might, nor by power, but it is by the spirit of the living God (Zach 4:6), that we will be able to take a natural person and bring them into spiritual maturity.

Perfecting can also be translated "equipping" or "preparing." Like the pastor, the main role of the evangelist is to help believers to identify their gifts, help to equip them in developing those gifts, and then release them into ministry. One of the reasons that the church has not grown is because the members are either not edified, or, they are being edified, but are not given opportunities to serve. The purpose of being edified is for service. All believers are called and given some kind of ministry for service.

For the work of the ministry: The gift of the evangelist is to manifest the gifts that God has given him. The passage in Ephesians 5 instructs us to use this gift in the world and within the church (unto the work of the ministry, and unto the building up of the body of Christ). Jesus' main purpose of coming to this world was to save the lost; therefore, the work of the ministry is to reach the world. "For God so loved the world that he gave his only begotten Son…" (John 3:16). God's plan for the believers in ministry is that through us the world might come to know Jesus Christ.

We are so far from this truth when we believe that we should separate ourselves from the world and remain within the walls, having a glorious time while we wait for the world to come and knock on our door. After all, didn't God promise in His Word that He will draw all men unto Himself? We take the Scripture so often out of its context. We must not separate the other part of the verse that says 'if I (Christ) be lifted up then I will draw all men unto myself.' How are they going to come in unless we go and lift up Christ to them? We were not told to stay but were commissioned to go to the world; to the lost world, the sick world, and the spiritually dying world. Jesus said to them, "Go ye into all the world and preach the gospel to every creation." (Mark 16:15). The Scriptures also say in Matt. 5:14-16 that, "Ye are the light of the world. A city that is set on a hill cannot be hid…" Why do we try to hide the light behind the walls? Light was designed to shine. If we were truly shining the light, we wouldn't even have to give an invitation for some one to attend our church; the light would shine brightly enough for people to follow us home.

Let's take a deeper look at an Evangelist:

With all that has been said earlier, it does appear that every believer is called to evangelize. *All believers are called to evangelize; however, not every believer holds the office of an evangelist.* The word "evangelist" is derived from the Greek work "euaggelion," which is translated; "to preach or to preach the Good News." The evangelist's ministry is predominately a preaching ministry. This entails preaching the Gospel in season and out of season. Paul's admonition to Timothy, "PREACH the word; be instant in season, out of season; reprove, rebuke, exhort with all longsuffering and doctrine." (II Timothy 4:2, emphasis mine).

Evangelist in Scripture

1. God Himself is the ultimate evangelist. Galatians 3:8 says, "And the scripture, foreseeing that God would justify the heathen through faith, preached before the gospel unto Abraham, saying, In thee shall all nations be blessed."
2. Jesus Christ was an evangelist, for He also "preached the gospel." "And it came to pass, that on one of those days, as he taught the people in the temple, and preached the gospel" (Luke 20:1). "And Jesus went about all the cities and villages, teaching in their synagogues, and preaching the gospel of the kingdom, and healing every sickness and every disease among the people" (Matthew 9:35).
3. In Acts 2, Peter preached a bold message that was primarily delivered to Jews. Peter was an evangelist.
4. Paul was an evangelist as well as an apostle (Rom 1:15).
5. John the Baptist was an evangelist, "In those days came John the Baptist, preaching in the wilderness of Judea, And saying, Repent ye: for the kingdom of heaven is at hand" (Matthew 3:1-2).
6. Philip the deacon was an evangelist (Acts 21:8).
7. Timothy the pastor was an evangelist (2 Tim 4:5).
8. All the early disciples, were scattered abroad went everywhere preaching the Word (Acts 8:4).
9. Paul and Barnabas preached: Paul and Barnabas journeyed to Antioch in Pisidia, where many Jews and Gentiles accepted the Word of God and believed after hearing them preach.

The Evangelist who hold the office:
- Preaching is their principle ministry
- Their preaching is focused on bringing people to a divine ultimatum
- They are ideal for revival work
- Evangelists have an intense burden to see the unsaved come into the fold
- They are moved with great boldness
- Very convincing, there is much power and authority in their preaching
- Often signs and wonders accompany their ministry
- They are prayer warriors
- Regardless of what text they choose from Scripture for their message, they have the ability to turn their message into a message of salvation
- Evangelists are often uncomfortable sitting at ease in Zion; they often have the desire to travel with the Gospel
- They usually bring people to salvation and then leave them for the local church to nurture them
- They don't make great pastors because their messages are often salvation messages. The saved need to hear more than that, as they are already saved. They leave something for the pastor to work with
- Evangelists are also engaged in the ministry of pastoral support; they work alongside the pastor in building up the local church. Assist in growth and edification
- They are very good encouragers both to the pastors, members and also to anyone they are in contact with. The evangelist stirs believers to win souls

Characteristics of an evangelist in general
- compassionate
- caring
- confident—that Jesus has the ability to set people free

- emulates the example of Christ
- obeys God's commission
- relies upon God's power and strength
- trusts in God
- a true witness
- proclaims the Gospel
- accomplishes God's will

5

THE POWER FOR MINISTRY

We were not only sent to preach the Gospel, but we are provided with an equipping agent, the power of God (anointing). The power of God in believers should be impacting the world. Why? Because there is a great need for the activation of the power of God in our homes, churches, communities, and in the nations. We are in a crisis hour; we are in a spiritual war zone; everyday, people are dying and going to hell; people are trapped in mental prisons, and disease is on the rampage. People are depressed, oppressed and perplexed. Satan's troops have entered our churches and are warring against the believers. It is a shame to admit that they are having a field day. Keep in mind that Jesus told us that He will build His church and the gates of hell will not prevail against it.

What are evangelists doing in the world? People nation-wide are in despair because the forces of darkness are working hard. Principalities, powers, and rulers of the darkness of this world have set up their camp and are at every side fighting against us. It is a disgrace that most of us are at ease in Zion. A high percentage of Christians are operating with a form of Godliness, but are denying its' power (2 Timothy 3:5). Many of our motives in ministry are wrong. It is all about me, myself, and I. We are seeking fame, money and power, having no concern for others. It is not about us, it is all about God. It is time we wake up, shake ourselves off, and do the will of God. We are to be a light in this dark world, but sadly, some believers have joined with the darkness.

Let us look at the purpose of the anointing. Luke 4:18 states, "The Spirit of the Lord is upon me, because he hath anointed me to preach the gospel to the poor; he hath sent me to heal the brokenhearted, to preach deliverance to the captives, and recovering of sight to the blind, to set at liberty them that are bruised." The word "anointed" means to rub. In the

Old Testament, individuals were anointed with the rubbing of oil. Today we are anointed because Christ rubs Himself on us and in us. God is a spirit; therefore, we are rubbed with His Spirit. Anointing sets us apart for certain tasks. Jesus knew we needed help to carry out His tasks because we are powerless on our own. This is why Jesus said, "I will send the comforter." The Holy Spirit's job is to work through us. He is the one who supplies the power.

Although Luke 4:18 was referring to Jesus Christ, it is also for us today. Jesus set the example for us so that we could carry on with His mantle. In Christianity, there is only one body and we as believers are part of that body, the body of Christ. The word "Christ" means "anointed one." Christ is the Messiah, the Son of God, "the anointed one." Everyone who is born again is anointed because we are all in Christ, "the anointed one." It doesn't matter how insignificant we might feel. We can rest assured that Christ is referring to all believers. All are special to God and are a part of the plan to carry out His task. He is not referring to certain people, but to all of His children. In the past, limitations might have been placed upon us by others, even by those that hold high positions in the church. Today I am here to declare the Word which said we are anointed with the power which will enable us to preach the Gospel, to deliver and set captives free. It doesn't matter what people say. If Christ says it that settles it. As a matter a fact, we can't do anything on our own, but with Christ we can do endless things. I had experienced the power of God richly on my life a couple of years ago and subsequently had a deep desire to preach. I wasn't aware of this passage (Luke 4:18), so I asked a pastor with whom I was acquainted if she thought that I was called to preach, and she told me that I was not. For years I refused to walk in the calling of God because I thought preaching wasn't for me. If I had known this truth then as I know now, I would have been much farther ahead. Today, our eyes have been opened and we do not need to get a second opinion. Let us read the Word for ourselves and believe that it is talking about us. It doesn't matter if we preach from the pulpit to thousands or at the grocery store to only one, we are still called to preach, deliver and set people free because it is not we who are going to accomplish it, but Christ in us and through us.

As we read earlier, not only is the Spirit of the Lord upon us, but we are also given the purpose of the anointing. The passage also tells us that <u>the purpose of the anointing</u> is to preach the Gospel, to be a witness, and share the Gospel. Having the anointing and not preaching is like staying in the upper room with the power and not going through the exit door. Can you imagine what would have happened if Peter remained in the upper room and did not preach? Look at the impact one man made in society. People are still being saved through Peter's preaching today. The anointing followed down through the pages of history. The anointing is a supernatural equipping agent to perform work, which in turn, will set people free. The anointing is not just to say that we have it so we can put it on a shelf like you would a trophy. It is not so we can be prideful. The anointing is not for emotional activities like shaking in the Spirit, or so we can have a good time without any passion or love for the unsaved. It is not for speaking in tongues so that we look powerful. *It is to edify the body of Christ*; we cannot accomplish anything without the anointing. All of Jesus' miracles and healings were done after He received the anointing.

The anointing serves many purposes; however, the main purpose for the anointing is for mankind. God loves mankind and that's why He came. This is why He stated clearly; to set others free and deliver them. Although we also have the authority through Christ to set ourselves free, the text does not say to set ourselves free but to set others free. What is the use of saying that we are anointed when we have no concern for others or no desire to win souls? The anointing will get results." We are to be a vessel for Christ, a channel of the anointing to the unsaved throughout the world; we need to allow God's anointing to flow through us to set people free, to bring deliverance and healing to the world around us.

The Scriptures goes further to say, "And these signs shall follow them that believe; In my name shall they cast out devils; they shall speak with new tongues; They shall take up serpents; and if they drink any deadly thing, it shall not hurt them; they shall lay hands on the sick, and they shall recover" (Mark 16:17-18). When we take a good look at Christendom, do we really see evidence of these verses? Maybe 'yes' in some isolated cases, but on a whole 'no,' otherwise there would not be such a great need for revival. Can you imagine if we take our stand and allow the Lord to manifest His power, what effect that would cause in this society?

There is no doubt that believers are equipped to fulfill the purposes of God, but we need to ignite the power. You see, there is dynamite sitting in the pews, singing in the choir, preaching and teaching behind the pulpit. Yet nothing is happing; why not? One of the reasons is because they refuse to ignite the power. The Word of God reassures us that He provides us with power and helps to accomplish the task. It doesn't matter how good we can sing, preach, and pray. It is of no effect without the anointing. For the power of the anointing to flow, we must be plugged into the source. Light cannot shine unless it is plugged into an electric source. So it is with the anointing. For it to work, it must be plugged into the Almighty power source (Jesus Christ). Caution, though! Remember that no form of sin is compatible with this source. If you are not right with God, there will be no power connection to you and if attempt to plug yourself in without repentance you could damage yourself greatly.

6

Evangelist in Revival

What is revival?

Revival is a renewing in our relationship with God where we place Him first. God must be first in our thoughts, in our time, in all our resources and in our daily lives. Revival can also be defined as: God spontaneously awakening His people by the Holy Spirit. As a result, His people will humble themselves, seek God's face, and **repent** from their sins. Outcome: God heals us from our spiritually dead state and reconnects us back to Himself, where we will experience the benefits of God. We will be willing to walk according to His ways with great joy.

Revival is:

   a. God's divine work among His people and the unsaved. (Hab. 3:2).
   b. When the human spirit experiences a fresh, new life.
   c. Man repent and God restores His Spirit to His people (Romans 11:29).

How to tell if you need a Spiritual Revival

1. There is deadness and apathy towards God and the things of God (Mt. 13:15)
2. Lacking feeling or sensitivity to God
3. Not having the capacity to live the Christian life
4. Not having the capacity to function in the Spirit, or the ability to sustain spiritual life; spiritual barrenness (Isa 59:1-2)
5. Not spiritually productive
6. Spiritually inactive; dormant

7. The Holy Spirit is seldom or no longer in operation in the church or your personal life
8. Devoid of spiritual activity
9. No freedom
10. Little or no sign of the fruit of the Spirit in your life. No peace, no joy, no happiness
11. No immunity to the Devil and the things of the Devil
12. Great love for the things of the world
13. Sin is dominant in the church and/or your personal life

Need For Revival in Scriptures

Nehemiah 4:2: "And he spake before his brethren and the army of Samaria, and said, what do these feeble Jews? Will they fortify themselves? Will they sacrifice? Will they make an end in a day? Will they **revive** the stones out of the heaps of the rubbish which are burned?"

Psalm 85:6: "Wilt thou not **revive** us again: that thy people may rejoice in thee?"

Hosea 6:2: "After two days will he **revive** us: in the third day he will raise us up, and we shall live in his sight."

Psalms 71:20: "Thou, which hast shewed me great and sore troubles, shalt **quicken** me again, and shalt bring me up again from the depths of the earth."

Psalm 118:17: "I shall not die, but **live**, and declare the works of the LORD."

Psalm 119:25: "My soul cleaveth unto the dust: **quicken** thou me according to thy word."

Psalm 119:37, "Turn away mine eyes from beholding vanity; and **quicken** thou me in thy way."

Psalm 119:40: "Behold, I have longed after thy precepts: **quicken** me in thy righteousness."

Psalm 143:11: "**Quicken** me, O LORD, for thy name's sake: for thy righteousness' sake bring my soul out of trouble."

Ezekiel 37:3: "And he said unto me, Son of man, can these bones **live**? And I answered, O Lord GOD, thou knowest."

Amos 5:4: "For thus saith the LORD unto the house of Israel, Seek ye me, and ye shall **live**."

Amos 5:14: "Seek good, and not evil, that ye may **live**: and so the LORD, the God of hosts, shall be with you, as ye have spoken."

I Corinthians 15:45: "And so it is written, the first man Adam was made a living soul; the last Adam was made a **quickening** spirit."

Romans 6:11: "Likewise reckon ye also yourselves to be dead indeed unto sin, but alive unto God through Jesus Christ our Lord."

Romans 8:13: "For if ye **live** after the flesh, ye shall die: but if ye through the Spirit do mortify the deeds of the body, ye shall **live**."

Galatians 2:20: "I am crucified with Christ: nevertheless I **live**; yet not I, but Christ **liveth** in me: and the life which I now **live** in the flesh I **live** by the faith of the Son of God, who loved me, and gave himself for me." (italics mine).

We need an explosive revival in our nation, the type of revival that will turn churches upside down, so that the explosion would overflow into the world and break the hard hearts of the hell-destined sinner.

One of the keys to this is old-fashioned, anointed preaching. The kind of preaching that causes men to weep, turn from their wicked ways and come to the Lord in sincerity.

Individuals in Scriptures whose preaching resulted in revival

Many believe today that there can be revival without evangelistic preaching. Yes, all things are possible with God. However, He chooses to use mankind in His great commission plan. We are all called to preach. However, some are anointed differently. "How shall they believe in him of whom they have not heard? And how shall they hear without a preacher?" (Romans 10:14). I am sorry to say that there are too many convenient preachers today; those who refuse to walk in the anointing. You may disagree with me and even blame the lack of results on the ones who are hearing the Word. Yes, in some cases, the receiver is at blame, but there is no sin that is more powerful than the Word of God when it is delivered with the supernatural power-packed anointing. Not all will be saved. The Bible says in Revelation that some will still remain filthy. Nevertheless, the Gospel is mighty to save but it must be delivered with the anointing.

God has always used anointed evangelists to carry out our great revivals. If we look back in Scripture we can attribute many great revivals to those who did the work of an evangelist. These men were anointed and set apart for God's work. For example:

- Nineveh experienced revival through Jonah's preaching.
- The great revival at Pentecost was a result of Peter's preaching.
- The great revival at the Jordan River was a result of John the Baptist's preaching. He preached, "Repent, for the Kingdom of Heaven is at hand." In those days many repented at the preaching of John the Baptist from Jerusalem, Judea and the regions around the Jordan River.

Preaching that will cause revival

As you read, keep the following in mind: Repentance is simple "turning." Preaching should never have the intention of bringing judgment on anyone. Preaching should not call down fire and brimstone on anyone. Repentance messages that are preached in ignorance will do more harm that good. Repentance should be preached in love at all times.

Now let's look at preaching that will cause revival

Any evangelistic preaching that does not include an echo call for repentance is not the true gospel! People are heading down the wrong path and have no desire to turn to God. The Gospel needs to be preached to them, telling them that they need to turn in the right direction. They need to turn to God and then do works that will benefit "repentance." There cannot be reconciliation without repentance. Wherever sin is, the message of repentance must be preached. Jesus told us in Luke 13:3, "except ye repent, ye shall all likewise perish." Why are we afraid to tell it like Jesus did? Jesus was not afraid to preach it. He preached the message of repentance. God commanded mankind everywhere to repent (Acts 17:30). This is the reason Jesus came, to call all sinners to repentance (Matthew 9:13). This Gospel is not new or strange. On the day of Pentecost, Peter commanded the people to repent; John the Baptist declared, "Repent, for the kingdom of heaven is at hand;" Jesus disciples went out two by two, "preaching that men should repent" (Mark 6:12). We cannot pretty it up; the truth is the truth and it needs to be proclaimed.

If you study the preaching of Jesus, you will recognize that His major theme was repentance (Mark 6:1) and this theme still continues today. The ultimate purpose for Christ's coming to earth was so that mankind would turn from their sinful ways (repent) and accept the gift of salvation. Scriptures instruct us to preach repentance. Luke 24:46-47 tells us that repentance must be preached to all nations. Acts 17:30; the message of repentance should be preached to both the Jews and Gentiles. The disciples followed Jesus' instruction; "And they went out, and preached that men should repent" (Mark 6:12). We too need to follow as they did. Many people view a 'repentance' message as negative. However, Jesus said it best in Luke 15:10, "there is joy in the presence of the angels of God over one sinner that repents."

The reason we are not effective in our preaching is because we are not proclaiming the message that Christ instructed us to proclaim. When we look back in the Scriptures, we see that the mission of the disciples - to win souls - was very effective because they obeyed the commission of Christ.

There are many kinds of preaching that produce results in the lives of believers. However, there is a special preaching that will bring sinful man to their knees, resulting in revival. This kind of preaching has always been the old-time anointed, supernatural power-packed preaching that was done with conviction. Jesus, Peter, Paul, John the Baptist, Elijah, and Jonah are all good examples of this style of preaching. This kind of preaching is not based on one's own opinion, but is based on the pure inspiration of Scripture. We see this kind of preaching in our society back in the old days. The men could preach and were highly anointed because they spent much time in prayer. Today in the church, we find many convenient messages. Today's messages are all about prosperity, joy, peace, total fulfillment, sowing seed, and on and on and on. Yes, most of these are part of the package, but they are not the full Gospel. A message of convenience was not why Jesus left His throne in glory; nor is it the message He instructed us to preach. The true message is about salvation; His theme is "repentance."

The law falls into the category of repentance. Many people think that because of grace the law has been done away with, and do not understand that without the law, there can be no salvation. The law is so vital; it is what speaks to the conscience of the sinner. Romans 1 explains that the law is the power of God unto salvation. Ps 19:7 says that the law of the Lord is perfect, converting the soul. The law tells us that we are in violation of God's standards and that no salvation can be accomplished in an unsaved person's life without repentance. Repentance means to turn from sin. The Ten Commandments are all about repentance. Why are preachers afraid to preach about repentance? Many people will hear the Gospel preached and understand repentance but have not truly repented. This is why we have so many unsaved within the church - religious but lost. (Luke 8:13).

The theme of many great revival messages in Scripture again is repentance; repent, repent, and repent. The men who preached these messages also practiced what they preached and were faithful in obeying 2 Chronicles 7:14, which says, "If my people, which are called by my name, shall humble themselves, and pray, and seek my face, and turn from their wicked ways; then will I hear from heaven, and will forgive their sin, and will heal their land." God often gave these preachers specific instructions to preach repentance.

Revival in Korea- Rev. Jae Rock Lee reported that, "Up until now, we have been experiencing revival by the power of the Holy Spirit in South Korea; but those pastors who had manifested the power of God passed away one by one and the revival seems to be stagnant and even it is decreasing gradually." Here again we see men who have been set apart being used to bring about revival. The three attributes that caused revival in Korea were: pastors that manifested the power of God, *cell groups, and intercessory prayer.*

Revival is up to God. God is up to the challenges of revival since the fall of mankind. It is man's responsibility to be ready for revival.

2 Chronicles 7:13-14 is the key to revival. "If my people, which are called by my name, shall humble themselves, and pray, and seek my face, and turn from their wicked ways; then will I hear from heaven, and will forgive their sin, and will heal their land."

Human's responsibility in Revival

-Humble yourself-pride will prevent us from going down on our knees. We cannot enter God's presence without humility. In order to be forgiven of our sins, we need to be humble. God will have nothing to do with pride and boastfulness. Pride will block our prayers from being answered. Therefore, pride must go before we even attempt prayer. As a result of pride, Satan was not able to communicate with God anymore. Although prayer has many mechanisms, let us understand that prayer is simply communicating with God.

-Pray-when we talk about prayer, we are not talking about prayers like "Gentle Jesus, meek and mild," or "Bless me! Bless me! Bless me!" Instead, let us say prayers whereby we come out of the natural, out of our sinful ways, pass through hell, terrorize the enemy's camp, having the Holy Spirit with us, and enter into the throne room of God. This type of prayer can be characterized as warfare prayer. We can also classify this as intercessory prayer because this type of prayer won't be selfish as it reveals the need to pray for others.

-Seek God's face- This does not mean the literal face of God. No one can look at God's face and live. This term is a metaphor. Seeking God's face in this passage (to my knowledge) is seeking His presence. We can seek the Lord in the natural, but it is only in His throne room that we can truly seek His face. Seeking God's face reveals His true identity; His face is where you experience great reward. You will never experience God's face outside of His throne room. He is too holy to live anywhere else. Do you catch the drift? God will set up His throne room if you prepare the place. Your heart can be God's throne room, but is it clean enough for God to enter? God inhabits the praises of His people. This simply says that He occupies this kind of environment. Although Moses was in the wilderness, he experienced God's face while he was in God's throne room. What am I talking about? I am talking about a deep spiritual encounter with God's presence that causes a man to hide his face from God. Don't forget that before man's fall in the Garden of Eden, Adam and Eve were able to see God's glory but their sin separated them from that benefit. Thanks be to God for this glorious privilege being made available again through Jesus Christ. In this we can ask God to intervene on behalf of the unsaved and He will create many opportunities.

-Turn from their wicked ways- The throne room experience will cause us to truly turn from our wicked ways and not to be burdened with the yoke of sin anymore. It is only through God's eyes that we can truly see the debt of our sins and understand the need to be completely changed.

When Isaiah had this experience, he recognized that he was filthy. Isaiah 6:1-8 says, "I saw also the LORD sitting upon a throne, high and lifted up, and his train filled the temple… Woe is me! for I am undone; because I am a man of unclean lips, and I dwell in the midst of a people of unclean lips: for mine eyes have seen the King, the LORD of hosts." In order for us to make a difference in this world, we have to be changed first. Christ said in His Word, "And I, if I be lifted up from the earth, I will draw all men to myself". If we as believers would turn from our wicked ways, then unbelievers will see Christ in us and they would have no choice but to accept Him. Our sins hide the glory of God in our lives.

It is important that we pay attention to the context of what God is saying in *2 Chronicles 7* as well as any other chapter of the Bible. I believe that the church as a whole often overlooks an entire passage and focuses its attention on what it wants to see. For example, in this passage, the focus with many churches is only "prayer." This is why we see no results. In this passage, there is a formula that needs to be followed and if followed correctly, we will see results. God is saying to humble ourselves. How many of us are truly humble? Then He said to pray. Yes, we pray and God hears us, but when we don't seek His face and turn from our wicked ways, we will not see His promises fulfilled. God's promises are always sure. His promises are already released in the spiritual realm, but for them to be made manifest in the natural, God's requirements must be met. This passage does work but only if it is followed in its entirety. If you look back through the Scriptures you will see that it works over and over again. For instance, the children of Israel turned from their wicked ways and God healed their land. God promised that if they would return to Him, He would heal them from their backsliding (Jeremiah 3:14). "I will heal their backslidings. I will love them freely." (Hosea 14:4).

-**Faith**–After we humble ourselves, pray, seek His face and turn from our wicked ways, we must believe that God can do His part. What is His part? It is His promises!

GOD'S PROMISES:

- **INCREASE**- *God has a harvest that is ripe* -"The harvest truly is plenteous, but the laborers are few; pray you therefore the Lord of the harvest, that he will send forth laborers into his harvest." (Matt 9:36- 38).

- **ANSWER**-He will hear from heaven, and He will forgive their sins (2 Chronicles 7:14). Do you know that someone somewhere prayed for you to come into the fold? There is a mystery in prayer that only God understands. I do know that when the righteous pray, the Lord hears. James 5:14-15 says, "Is any sick among you? let him call for the elders of the church; and let them pray over him, anointing him with oil in the name of the Lord: And the prayer of faith shall save the sick, and the Lord shall raise him up; and if he have committed sins, **they shall be forgiven him.**" Notice how forgiveness is somehow wrapped up in the prayer. "The righteous cry, and the LORD heareth, and delivereth them out of all their troubles" (Psalm 38:17). God is so awesome! "For the eyes of the Lord are over the righteous, and his ears are open unto their prayers..." (I Peter 3:12). "For the eyes of the Lord are over the righteous, and his ears are open unto their prayers: but the face of the Lord is against them that do evil." (Proverbs 15:8). "I will strengthen Judah and save the tribes of Joseph. I will restore them because I have compassion on them. They will be as though I had not rejected them, for I am the LORD their God and I will answer them." (Zechariah 10:6).

- **HEALING**-He will heal their land - when God heals our land we will notice it. Some parts of Korea are experiencing a healing right now and it is so noticeable that the news is being spread abroad. What is this healing? It is revival. Two attributes of this revival in Korea are cell groups and intercessory prayer. I am sure that they are praying, and that their prayers are effective. I am also sure that they are following the formula we read earlier. One of the things preventing us from praying effective prayers is that we have no time to spend in prayer. The cares of life have taken up our prayer time. We don't even have time to pray for ourselves, never mind our unsaved family and not to mention, the world. Well then! How are we going to experience great revivals? Notice in the Scriptures, that the many signs and wonders that Jesus performed were as a result of prayer. He spent much time in prayer and little time actually performing those mighty works. What if we adopted the same principle today? Do you think we would have many results? Of course! Jesus promised that we would do even greater works. He has not changed. He may not be here today in the flesh, but in the Spirit He is willing to work through us if we make ourselves available.

It is always God's desire to bring revival but He cannot hear us because we are far from him. Jesus is pure holiness and as the book of Psalms says 'if iniquity is in the heart, he will not hear us.' Isaiah 59:2 says, "But your iniquities have separated between you and your God and your sins have hid his face from you, that he will not hear." You might say, "I don't have any iniquity." Do you realize that it could be a little sin such as refusing to preach the Gospel, by being a witness? Disobedience is sin. Sometimes we are not even aware that we are in sin, but we could be and one of the signs might be that our prayer has no effect.

Nevertheless, God is also a God of love who loves us so much that if we turn away from our sins, He promises that He will forgive us. He is a God who doesn't lie, His promises are yea and amen, and He will never goes back on His promises. It is up to us to make a change. People are so reluctant to step out because they think that they alone can't make a difference. That is so far from the truth. The Word of God says, one can chase a thousand…one is a majority. Can you imagine if every one said that someone else can make a difference? No one would be impacted with the Gospel. It only takes one to make a difference in this world. The Bible also says that we are the light of the world. Do you realize the impact of light? Take for example natural light: when one little light bulb shines, it is quite visible for a distance, it serves many purposes and ultimately, changes the darkness around it. If natural light has such capability, imagine the spiritual light that we are able to produce through Christ, which will cause tremendous results. Let us begin the work of revival in us and others will be impacted as a result.

When we are in line with God's plan, not only will we be a light set on a hill but we will also have the burden to pray for the land so that it too would come to repentance and God would heal their land.

God will never fail to give what He promised (a harvest of souls). He promised us that He would build His church. We are part of that building plan. Many souls will be saved when we take up our responsibilities and let God do the rest. Evangelism is about us coming out from behind the city walls and going into the surrounding fields and begin reaping the harvest that God has provided.

God is up to revival since the fall of man

Soon after creation, mankind sinned and lost maximum life. Not only were humans deprived of a perfect paradise, but they also lost their physical and spiritual connection to God. They literally lost everything as a result of their disobedience. However, we do not need to remain in such a predicament. We can be revived and remain revived until we leave this sin-contaminated world. Let's see how this can happen and what opportunities we have to be revived. Genesis 3:15 says, "And I will put enmity between you and the woman, and between your offspring and hers; he will crush your head, and you will strike his heel."

The seed of the woman is Jesus Christ. Man does not have to live in sin because Jesus has already bruised the head of the serpent by dying for our sins. Sin and death have been defeated forever. John 3:16 says, "For God so loved the world…"

"The Cross is God's incredible magnet by which multitudes of men and women who were far removed from the Lord by their rebellion and sinfulness have been drawn into an intimate, loving relationship with Him.

In 1Timothy 2:4 we read that God desires that all men might be saved and come to knowledge of the truth. He loves all men equally and unconditionally (John 3:16) and is not willing that any should perish (2 Peter 3:9). He is constantly and, by various means, drawing men to Himself. At times God has used the preaching of the gospel to awaken people to their need of salvation, while at other times He may permit some difficulty, a sickness or tragedy, or even a feeling of emptiness to bring them to Himself. At other times Christians can be God's "magnet", drawing others to the Lord by their consistent, godly lifestyle. Unfortunately, Satan does his utmost to quench God's drawing power with counter attractions".[3]

John 6:44: "No man can come to me, except the Father which hath sent me draw him."

He who plants, he who waters, and He who gives the increase

Paul and Apollos were very involved in evangelism. They were the two evangelists who helped to establish the church in Corinth. In 1 Corinthians 3:6 the apostle Paul says, "I planted the seed, Apollos watered it, but God

---

3 Pastor Davies, torchbearers-for-christ.org

has been making it grow." This passage acknowledges the planter and the one who waters, but the credit goes to the one who causes the seed to grow – God. Therefore, it is important to trust God and play our part in the harvesting while being aware that it is up to God to bring the increase. It is our responsibility to plant and water while we wait on God to bring the increase.

It is God who saves

It is God who saves. Mankind can only operate from one power source - God. Without God's strength, men are not only spiritually dead, but also are physically dead. Humans can't save anyone, but with God's strength they are able to do the impossible. "Then Jesus said to his disciples, "Truly I tell you, it is hard for someone who is rich to enter the kingdom of heaven. Again I tell you, it is easier for a camel to go through the eye of a needle than for someone who is rich to enter the kingdom of God." When the disciples heard this, they were greatly astonished and asked, "Who then can be saved?" Jesus looked at them and said, "With man this is impossible, but with God all things are possible." (Matt 19:23-26). It looks impossible for some hard, rebellious unbelievers to come to Christ with our human understanding, but it is easy for God. Therefore, we are to be encouraged that our duty is to do our part but only God can do the saving.

The Evangelist is one of the most important keys to revival

-True evangelists are called and anointed by God, particularly for the purpose of evangelizing.

-They are in the New Testament plan to carry out the Great Commission.

-Not just any kind of preaching can cause a revival: but the preaching that will cause the people of God to be revived, get them on praying ground, help them become endued with soul-winning power, and convict and convert hardhearted sinners is a certain kind of preaching that marks God's anointed evangelist.

-They also preach the kind of message that gets Christians on track, and lays on their hearts the burden for soul-winning.

-The evangelist sees that the Gospel gets to the unsaved.

- Gets the Gospel to everywhere possible in the community, and to all the world.

What are the hindrances to Revival?

- **We have no time for the Holy Spirit in our congregation**—Church services must start at a certain time and end at a set time without any interruptions. Church service has become a ritual. We go to church with a program in place and ensure that it is carried out. We don't give any room for the Holy Spirit to move. Sinners often come to the church with broken hearts and during worship God is melting their hearts, but because of the programmed service, the melted hearts begin to re-solidify.

- **Insensitivity to What the Holy Spirit is doing in a Service**—A simple song can ignite the Holy Spirit to cause an explosion. Therefore, we need to be sensitive in what songs we select to sing for the hour. The Spirit of God can be quenched by the wrong song or music. If the service is going in another direction, (for example, a simple little member giving God praise in the spirit by speaking to God in tongues, or a word of knowledge coming forth), leaders often put out the fire by quenching the ignition.

- **Quenching the Holy Spirit**: The Holy Spirit is very sensitive. He will try to descend on an individual but if He is not welcome He will leave. Quenching the Holy Spirit is done by allowing the flesh to dominate and by preventing the Holy Spirit to take full preeminence. These things are evil and 1 Thess. 5:19-22 tells us to abstain from every form of evil which includes quenching the Holy Spirit. Spiritual things are foolishness to the natural man. Therefore if we do not understand the move of the Spirit it is best that we leave it. How I pray for discernment in the church!

- **Not enough anointing in the churches** and/or the church has a form of godliness, but denies the power thereof. We so often misinterpret emotion for anointing. Preaching very loud as if the entire church is deaf is not anointed. Speaking in many tongues is not always anointed, jumping over benches is not anointed…when one is truly anointed, the nine fruits of the spirit will be evident, and the gifts of the Spirit will also be in operation. We will see works with results.

- **Lack of prayer** or our prayers are empty words designed to impress others; prayer has become a ritual and an obligation. We are too caught up in the pleasures of this world and have no time for prayer.

- **Lack of love, unity and compassion.** People are so much in need of love today. They seek to find it in so many sources and are not able to find it. Not even in the church can you find much love. No wonder people are turned off from church/church people! If we truly have the love of God in our life, we would have no choice but to share it. Love can be a good weapon to use in witnessing. God's love is so penetrating that it can crack the hearts of hard hearted sinners and enter in. Love is very contagious and life changing. This love is able to contaminate whoever it comes in contact with. I am talking about the *agape* love. Do you have it? If you do, you don't have to wonder because it speaks volumes for itself. It cannot hide. Without love there cannot be any unity or compassion. How I wish for unity within the church! United we stand but divided we fall. When we are not in unity, we are in division and division is confusion. This is why we don't have revival. In the upper room on the day of Pentecost every one was in unity and as a result the Holy Spirit ascended. God is not the author of confusion and will not work in confusion. We need unity in the church as on the day of Pentecost so that revival fire can fall.

- **We are afraid to get emotional**—How can one experience the almighty power of God and not get emotional? It is normal to express our emotion when we watch a ball game, attend a rock concert, or win the lotto, but it is abnormal to get emotional when we are touched by God. I personally cannot understand it. The Scripture is full of emotionalism. Psalms 47:1 states, "***O clap your hands***, all ye people: ***Shout*** unto God with the voice of triumph." Psalms 149:3, "Let them praise his name in the ***Dance***: let them ***sing*** praises unto him with the ***Timbrel*** and ***harp***." It is quite okay to dance before the Lord with all our might. Even king David danced before the Lord. "Wearing a linen ephod, David was dancing before the LORD with all his might" (II Samuel 6:14). Are these few examples of emotional activities strange? Of course not! They are expressions that will cause the presence of God to be rich in our congregations, bring people down on repentant knees, causes them to be clean, and provides them with entrance into the heavenly realm, where the power of God can come down. The Bible says that when the praises go up then the blessing will come down. God inhabits the praises of His people. Healing and deliverance can take place in His presence. Yokes can be broken in His presence. What about crying, laughing, and leaping? Is this manifestation scriptural? Psalms 126:2, 3 says, "Our mouths were filled with laughter, our tongues with songs of joy.

Then it was said among the nations, The LORD has done great things for them. The LORD has done great things for us, and we are filled with joy" Also Luke 6:23 states, "Rejoice in that day, and *leap for joy*." Not only is the manifestation of the Spirit scriptural, we also hear of it in history. **John Wesley** (1703-91), the founder of the Methodist movement, was the most well-known revival preacher of his time. He reported that "people dropped on every side as thunderstruck as they fell to the ground, others with convulsions exceeding all description and many reported seeing visions. Some shook like a cloth in the wind, others roared and screamed or fell down with involuntary laughter."[4]

- **Fear**— Fear kept the man in the parable of the talent in Matthew 25:25, from using the talent that his master had entrusted to him: "And I was afraid, and went and hid thy talent in the earth: lo, there thou hast that is thine." *Fear was a hindrance to the disciples' faith also*. Matthew 8:26: "And he saith unto them, Why are ye fearful, O ye of little faith? Then he arose, and rebuked the winds and the sea; and there was a great calm." We are too afraid to preach the Gospel because we are afraid of criticism and rejection. We are too afraid to launch out in ministry because of agenda a, b, and c. Get a grip! The enemy is a liar. Fear will hinder the mighty hands of God to work in your life. Don't let fear rob you; overcome fear with faith, and step out into victory.

- **Fake Fire**—Satan uses fake fire. He uses all kinds of devices to keep us from the real fire. Watered-down preaching, false teaching, false prophets, cults, huge healing and deliverance ministries that are operating through his power, huge hip-hop/reggae gatherings, etc.

- **Unanswered prayer** because of sin - the Bible says that our iniquity will hinder us from hearing God. We can pray from now to eternity but if we do not turn from our sinful ways our prayer is going no where. We are wasting our time.

- **Sin**, gossip, love of money, the lust of the flesh, a critical spirit, and the list goes on— God will not be a part of the church that

---

4 pastorbrendan.wordpress.com/2010/08/26/manifestations-of-the-spirit-in-church-history-mike-bickle.

harbors sin; therefore, church is going on but without God. This is a dead church that is in deception. Jesus talked about all kind of hindrances in Scripture: "Evil thoughts, adulteries, fornications, murders, thefts, covetousness, deceit, lasciviousness, an evil eye, blasphemy, pride, foolishness: all these *evil things* come from within, and defile the man" (Mark 7:21-23). You might only be able to admit to one or more of the above, but unfortunately, all of the above are in what we call "church." Sin in the church is pushed under the carpet and yet we are praying for revival. Under these conditions revival will not happen. In today's society, morality has been twisted. Truth is now classified as wrong and wrong is now classified as truth. Good will always prevail; however, sin is accepted as good in the world and even among the churches.

- **Pride**— those that are prideful will believe that they are in need of nothing because they have everything (Revelation 3:17). They expect that you give them respect (I Timothy 6:4). Esther 3:5: They believe that they are better than everyone else. Luke 18:11: They are extremely proud of their accomplishments. Daniel 4:30: They believe that they are great. (Acts 12:22-23) God will not walk with the proud. The proud are alone and they are powerless. We need God. Pride comes before a fall and we are experiencing a fall right now; we need revival.

- **Spiritual Warfare** – Eph. 6:12 "For we wrestle not against flesh and blood, but against principalities, against powers, against the rulers of the darkness of this world, against spiritual wickedness in high places." The church might be somewhat aware of these powers but is mingling with them, as it is afraid of them and is not equipped to deal with them. These spirits are also very conniving and work in ways that we are not aware of. They are definitely having a field day with the believers in order to stop revival.

- **Lack of love for God**—we have created other gods beside the true and living God, some of which are earthly interests and occupations that are more important to us than the things of God. We are so caught up in TV, the internet, texting, sports, recreation, etc. rather than reading the Word of God and prayer.

- **Our focus is on numbers rather than conversion**—numbers will tickle our prideful desires and produce lots of money. Therefore, rather than having Holy Ghost prayer meetings, we go out of our way to have rock and roll gospel concerts that will draw bigger crowds.

- **Some of the leaders who are in authority do not meet scriptural qualifications.** Many people are in leadership positions for different reasons: degrees, friendship, eloquent speech, for money, anything else besides God. Again you find people in authority who have no connection to God; their lifestyle is not up to Biblical standards, they are spiritually immature, in the wrong office... The flesh is an obstacle to the move of the Holy Spirit. It takes an anointed, called-out one to effectively do the works of God. Flesh will embrace sin, flesh will give Satan room, flesh will stand in God's way, and flesh won't accomplish anything supernatural... flesh is a major blockage to revival.

- **Not following God's instruction book (the Bible)-**There are solutions for everything on the face of the earth in this book and if followed correctly, will have absolute effect. Unfortunately, we are seeing the opposite because man has strayed away from the Word of God immensely, especially in these last days. On a large scale, the Word of God is either being discarded, abandoned, misinterpreted, or manipulated. Mankind has twisted the Word to suit themselves and have also diluted it to please others.

- **Most believers are at ease in Zion (bring complacency within the church)** and make no effort to witness to the lost. There are a great percentage of believers that have no consciousness of love for the lost. How are they going to believe unless we tell them about the Gospel?

7

There is Power in Prayer

Prayer is such an important key to revival. If we look back in history, we will see that prayer was the ignition to every revival explosion. Prayer was the key behind the many powerful evangelists that were used by God.

The Bible says that if the righteous call on Him he will hear them.

As was mentioned earlier, the harvest is plentiful, but the workers are few. We do not have to ask God to create a harvest for us, what we need is an opportunity to reap the harvest. God told us in His Word that there is already a harvest ready to be reaped. It is not only our responsibility to go and reap it but also to pray for labourers. We cannot reap such a great harvest alone. We need help because not only is it too large for us, it is a spiritual work and we are faced with principalities and power in high places.

Yes, we might have the skills to go out, but without prayer we are less effective and vulnerable to the enemy. Also, remember that it is men who sow and water but it is God who gives the increase (1 Cor. 3:6-7). We will do the possible but God is the one who will do the impossible.

You need to pray and ask God to give you:

Strength

Help to prepare the hearts of the unsaved

Love

Insight

Compassion for the lost

Desire to witness

Boldness

The authority to bind Satan (principalities, power and rulers in high places)

We must remember that when we go out into the harvest field we are embarking upon a field of the dead that need to come alive. The harvest field is like the field that Ezekiel saw in his vision.

The Valley of Dry Bones (Ezekiel 37:1-14)

God brought Ezekiel into a valley that was full of many dry bones. It seemed impossible for those dry bones to live. The Lord asked Ezekiel if he thinks those dry bones can live and he says, "O Lord GOD, thou knowest." Then God told him to "Prophesy unto these bones and say to them, O ye dry bones, hear the word of the LORD. Thus saith the Lord GOD unto these bones; Behold, I will cause breath to enter into you, and ye shall live: And I will lay sinews upon you, and will bring up flesh upon you, and cover you with skin, and put breath in you, and ye shall live; and ye shall know that I am the LORD."

Ezekiel did as the Lord commanded. And as he prophesied, "there was a noise, and behold a shaking, and the bones came together, bone to his bone. And when I beheld, lo, the sinews and the flesh came up upon them, and the skin covered them above: but there was no breath in them. Then said he unto me, Prophesy unto the wind, prophesy, son of man, and say to the wind, Thus saith the Lord GOD; Come from the four winds, O breath, and breathe upon these slain, that they may live. So I prophesied as he commanded me, and the breath came into them, and they lived, and stood up upon their feet, an exceeding great army."

Ezekiel 37:11-14, The Lord says to Ezekiel, "Son of man, these bones are the whole house of Israel: behold, they say, Our bones are dried, and our hope is lost: we are cut off for our parts. Therefore prophesy and say unto them, Thus saith the Lord GOD; Behold, O my people, I will open your graves, and cause you to come up out of your graves, and bring you into the land of Israel. And ye shall know that I am the LORD, when I have opened your graves, O my people, and brought you up out of your graves, and shall put my spirit in you, and ye shall live, and I shall place you in your own land: then shall ye know that I the LORD have spoken it, and performed it, saith the LORD."

As dead as those bones were in Ezekiel's vision, so are the unsaved in our society. These dead can only come back to life if God intervenes: therefore, it is of great importance that we ask the almighty God to raise the dead (the sinners) back to life through prayer. We have the power to prophesy through the Word of God. The Word is powerful and we can pray it over this dead world. Words are so powerful that when you decree a thing, according to the Bible, it shall come to pass. Not many understand the power of the spoken word. The Word was meant to be spoken. This universe was created as a result of the spoken word of God. In the beginning, God said "Let there be…and there was…" When we preach, we must understand the power of the spoken word. The Word has power to change lives.

Let's look at prayer in an overall scope

Prayer for many believers across the globe has become a performance, or ritual. One of the main reasons is that they find prayer to be of no effect, and as a result, causes misunderstanding, confusion, a lack of faith, and the lack of belief in God and His attributes. God is Changeless (Heb. 1:12); God is All Powerful (Gen. 18:25); God is All Knowing (Rom. 11:33); God is everywhere (Ps. 139:7-12); God is Eternal (2 Pet. 3:8); God is Holy (Is. 6:1-3); God is Righteous (Rom. 2:6-16); God is Love (Mark 10:18). Many Christians are living in defeat with no clue how to escape and what abundant blessing God desires for them to walk in. These blessings are sitting in the spiritual realm waiting to be released by what they regard as so ineffective - prayer. We blame so many things for the many problems we face, not realizing that the answers for our problems lie in prayer. Prayers for salvation for the world, revitalization, freedom from fear (Ps.118:-6), strength (Ps. 138:3), guidance and satisfaction (Is.58:9-11), wisdom and understanding (Dan. 9:20-27) deliverance from harm (Joel 2:32). Prayer is one of the most important tools in a Christian life. Once it is understood and used properly it will be very effective. We need to understand that God has designed prayer in order for us to have sweet communion with Him which will give us fulfillment.

When we pray, we are in the natural applying spiritual force that produces supernatural results which will be made manifest in the natural.

Many studies and the Word of God have proven that there is not a prayer that goes unanswered once it is lined up with the Word of God. It is God's desire to help us. He designed prayer so that in our communication with Him, we can ask and He will provide all our needs (Matt. 6:9-13). We must believe that our prayer is answered (Matt. 11:24), whether or not we see the manifestation of it right away. It is not for us to know the time when it will manifest; God knows when the time is right for us to receive an answer. We will view prayer differently when we understand that God cannot lie, nor does He have time to play hide and go seek with us. His promises are yea and amen. If He wasn't planning on answering, He wouldn't have told us to pray without ceasing.

From before the foundation of the earth, God had us in His blueprint (Rom 8:29). This plan was established in Genesis and was re-established at Calvary. Nothing can change this plan (Ps. 33: 11), however, we can choose to walk according to it or reject it. God has given us His law in His Word for us to follow; we can believe it or reject it. If we obey it, we will understand how we are to have fulfillment. God's Word tells us that we were given a spiritual nature like God, and if we refuse to walk according to this nature, we are in danger (Genesis 1:26-27). It also tells us that God is our only source and we are not able to live adequately without this connection. The fall of man proved this to be true (Genesis 1). God has given us power, dominion, and authority over the earth: however, we cannot tap into them without His help. This is why He provides prayer so that we can communicate with Him and so that He will direct, help and guide us. God trusted us to replenish and have dominion over the earth, but we have become blind and have lost sight of the truth of our position. We have allowed Satan to rule the earth for us rather than us ruling it through connection with God. We need to understand that Satan is only the god of this world until we take back our original position. For us to walk in our position, we need to know who God is and how He works, and His plans for us. We also need to know who we are, how we are to have dominion, the power we have through prayer, and our need for prayer. We need to be awakened not only to know our inheritance but also to walk in it; not by ourselves, but by faith in the Sovereign God. The book, "The Purpose and Power of Prayer" by Dr. Myles Munroe tells us that our need for prayer is a result of the way God has arranged dominion… it also tells us that "prayer is an earthly license for heavenly interference."[5] All

---

5 Dr. Myles Munroe, Understand the Purpose and Power of Prayer, Copyright 2002 by Dr. Myles Munroe. Library of Congress, Cataloging-in-Publication Data. Printed in USA pp 37, 38

our needs are locked up in our prayers. When we understand God's will and our purpose, we will pray with confidence, knowing that we are exercising the dominion God has given us. In this light, our prayer is guaranteed an answer. When we pray, we are involving ourselves with God and agreeing with God's purposes.

Our authority in prayer was lost because of our disconnection with God. Although we were given authority and dominion over the earth, we can only have it through God. To have such authority, we must be in one accord with God and this is why we were created in His image with His breath in us (Gen. 1:26-27). Our position tells me that God will never go back on His purpose and He indeed honours His Word above His name. In spite of our fall (Romans 6:2), God provided a plan through His Son Jesus Christ to redeem us (John 3:3, 7), and restore us to our original position so that His Word in the beginning will be established. Jesus is indeed God (John 1:1). In the beginning, we were made alive because God had blown His breath into us (Gen.1:26:27). We become dead when we sinned (Gen. 3 17-19). God provided Jesus, and by faith we become alive again spiritually (Rom.6:4; 2). If Jesus isn't God, then God changed His original plan. However, God cannot go back on His Word; therefore, redemption through Jesus proves that Christ is indeed God in us, the hope of glory (Col. 1:27). What an authority we have with the almighty God living in us! Our possibilities are endless, our power is untouchable and our authority is unquestioned. Through the Spirit, we are walking dynamically with heavenly authority. Jesus reclaimed our dominion and then set an example for how we are to have authority. Jesus kept in unity with His Father; He showed us that He was not here to do His own work but to do the work of God. In John 14, Jesus had a connection with God; therefore, His prayer was effective. Therefore, we are instructed to have this same kind of connection as Christ (Phil. 2:5).

When we look at the earthly side, we see how God had replaced Adam (Rom. 5:12-19; Gen. 3 1-17). We are no longer the seed of Adam but have been adopted by Jesus Christ and now we are sons and daughters of God (Eph. 1:5). Since we are children of the most High God, if we adopt His attributes, then we are rightfully heir to all that is His. The Psalms of David say, "The earth is the Lord's, and the fullness thereof..." We are no longer orphans but have been adopted into the family of a Holy King. Because this King is royalty, we too are part of the royal priesthood from the royal lineage (1 Pet. 2). We are not offspring of a king who has dominion over only one country, but a King who has dominion over the entire universe, both physically and spiritually. We have been made kings and priests to God and we shall reign on the earth (Rev. 5:10). We are no longer ordinary people, but a set-apart people of high caliber. When we look at the royal family, we can see that we are living like servants to a counterfeit king. When we see a king's palace, our mouths are open with awe. If this is the case with an earthly palace, how much greater is our King of Kings' Kingdom (Rev. 21)? It is out of this world; it must be breath taking. The Word of God says, "Thy kingdom come, thy will be done on earth." Even though we are on earth, God's kingdom can be here with us in the spiritual realm if we believe. That's why the Word says that we are in the world but not of the world (John 17:14-16). We have rights and privileges to enter into the resources of God through prayer (Matt. 18). God gave us the keys to the kingdom. We need to understand that we cannot tap into or release anything except through Jesus' Name (John 16). His Word has power and when the Word is in us, the authority will come forth. We will come alive through Him (John 5:7-9). "If ye abide in me, and my Word abide in you, you shall ask what ye will, and it shall be done unto you" (John 15:7). Jesus is the living Word that lived among us (John 1:14).

God is Holy (Is. 6 1:3), righteous (Deut 32:4), and just (Rom. 3:26). He is worthy of our honour, praise and respect (Phil 2:9-11). We cannot go into God's presence with any form of sin. We tend to abuse grace, not understanding that it is not a means to temporarily cover up sin, but to permanently wipe it out. God's grace is a permanent solution to bring us into God's presence. God is looking for sincere people who will receive His grace and not go back to their old sinful nature. God has justified us and declared us righteous like Him (Rom. 5:1). Because He has done us such a great favour, we are not to entangle ourselves anymore in the snare of sin, but show our love and appreciation to God by maintaining His righteousness. He deserves it since He is righteous (Lev. 20:26). Righteousness is the only way we can enter into the presence of God (Heb. 12:14). The Bible provides us with the whole armor to keep us clean (Eph. 6:11-20). We can maintain His righteousness through His Word and the connection we have (prayer). Our righteous position is: by faith we believe, acknowledging God's holiness, respecting it and living in it, knowing what God did to keep us connected to Him. When we give Him the glory that He rightfully deserves, we are acknowledging His power.

We are joint heirs with Christ's inheritance (Rom 8:27). The heir to the throne is not just for an individual or a group of people, but for all nations: Jews and Gentiles, male and female who by faith believe in Jesus Christ and are born into the kingdom of heaven. To enter God's presence, we cannot enter with bulls, rams, burnt offerings or sin offerings anymore, but we can cleanse ourselves by the Word (John 17:17), and by faith ask God to forgive us through Jesus Christ and enter in with the spotless Lamb in our hearts (1 Pet.1:18). When we are clean, praises of sweet-smelling fragrance will go up to God. This is the time in which we will have sweet communion with God. Therefore, we must separate ourselves from every distraction that would cause separation from God's presence. It doesn't matter where we are; as long as our hearts are clean we can be in God's presence (Ps. 24:3-4). After we have sought God diligently, we can now ask for whatever we need and He will grant it to us according to His Word (Ps. 24:5).

Many people are overflowing with love and are living a righteous life; they have taken steps to prevent themselves from going back to the life of sin. Entering God's presence is always easy for this group of people; they experience the joy of His presence and believe with all their hearts that they have met with God, and yet find out their prayer has not been answered. I myself have been there and because of a lack of knowledge, I have sometimes questioned what went wrong. To God be the glory! After studying Chapter 5 of Dr. Myles Munroe's book "Understanding the Purpose and Power of Prayer,"[6] I learned that it is not because I don't have faith, but as a matter of fact, I was created like God, therefore, live by faith. If that is really the truth, why then have my prayers not been answered? I have been in God's presence and have applied the Word (ask and I will receive). This chapter brought to my attention is that I might be using the wrong faith. After much examination on my part, I realized that I was indeed using negative faith which was a result of not knowing the depth of the Word. There were many negative influences around my life twisting the Word of God like Satan did to Eve in the garden (Gen. 1), and also to Jesus in the wilderness (Matt. 4:1-10). These influences would tell me it is impossible for it to work. By the way, why didn't I realize that faith means to believe in the impossible? It is negative to believe that it will not work. That's why I can understand the Scripture that says, life and death is in the power of the tongue (Proverbs 18:21). If we speak death, negative faith

---

6 ibid, pp 91-106

will release death and if we speak life, positive faith will release life. We speak so many negative things in our lives with negative faith and that's why we are living in such defeat. The Word of God has instructed us to decree a thing and it will come to pass (Job 22:28). Are we truly decreeing positive things by faith and waiting for it to come to pass? Our faith is very powerful because things are being released into our lives, except it is the negative things that we decree or believe. Many times I neglect the right kind of faith and allow the enemy to contaminate it with the negative faith. God's Word is true and if we hold on to the truth it will never fail. If we allow our hearts and mind to be unstable with all kinds of winds of doctrine, we will be carried away (Eph 4:14). For the positive faith to work, we must hold on to it and diminish all negative words and thoughts. We must also realize that only the faith that is lined up to the Word of God will work and not our own desire. Our desire may also be according to the Word of God, but it might not be good for us at the time we want it to work. If we hold on to faith, it will nourish what we believe and bring it in the right season.

Many Christians find it hard to spend time in prayer with God and yet desire miracles to happen for them. Time spent with God is very important. Spending time with God will eventually save time; we will gain wisdom, knowledge, understanding, guidance and power. The more time we have with God will make our work easier; we will find peace, joy and comfort. While we are with Him, He is working in the spiritual realm for us, breaking every chain, mending every trial and error and removing all spiritual wickedness in high places for us, so that when we depart from Him it will be very easy for us. After spending time with God and we come out of His presence, all we have to do is speak the Word and everything will come crashing down before our eyes. The word is powerful…Eph. 4:12. I believe we try too hard to fight the battle on our own since we are only flesh and bone which has no strength. All we need to do is seek God and He will do it for us. It is His desire to do it for us but we are not allowing Him to do it. God is the only sovereign God, the God of the impossible, and the source of all power. When we perform miracles, we are not the ones who do it. God has already done it for us and that's why we are not to take the glory for ourselves. We can only speak by the strength of God and then behold the manifestation before our eyes. We can't do anything, we are only agreeing with God. Is there any thing too hard for God to do? (Jer. 32:17). "No!" The reason why some situations seem hard to tackle is because we wait until we are faced with them before we seek the face of the Lord. I always wondered why the praise group at my previous church had to praise for more than two hours before God's presence appeared, and then I realized that they did not seek the Lord in the week or even the night before, and as a result, held up the service. What should have taken a minute, required two or more hours. Jesus is a key example for us; He spent more time with God and less time doing all His miracles.

There is much confusion over how we are to pray. Many have gone to the extremes of seeking other spirits to aid them, while others have gone to those whom they think have a special connection with God. We need no other advice or any new method on how we are to pray. If we go to Matthew 6 we will find the model prayer that will give us results. It teaches us how not to be selfish in prayer, it instructs us not only to go to God for ourselves, but also for others, and it teaches us how to approach God with honour and respect. Matthew 6 tells us how to agree with what God has already accomplished. This model prayer also shows us how to forgive others before we can be forgiven. At the end of the model prayer we can exercise faith by giving God thanks before our prayer manifests in the natural.

It is important for us to be silent before the Lord in prayer; this is where body, spirit, mind and emotion can come into oneness with God. When every distracting thought has been gotten rid of we are able to find His presence and connect with Him. We are now able to acknowledge Him as the mighty Redeemer, the sin Cleanser, the holy and righteous Judge. When we are in oneness we are able to give Him true adoration which prepares us for confession. We must allow Him to tell us what we need to confess. God knows everything, the deep secrets of our hearts (Ps. 44:21); we would be shocked to know what is hidden in there. At this point we allow Him to search us, mold us, and make us into perfect gold. God is the only one that can forgive sin; we are not able to do it ourselves. We are forgiven when we agree with God about the things that are in our hearts. When He reveals them, we must sincerely repent and not just pretend because we are caught red-handed. The fear of God should come upon us knowing that we have sinned against the sovereign God. He is so loving and kind to give us His attributes and we mess with it. Once all iniquity is rid from our hearts, we are sin free, there is nothing blocking us from God and His resources. At this point, God will accept our thanks and we can now offer unto God living sacrifices of praise for all that He has done for us. Sinful hearts will not give Him the praise He deserves. Only a pure heart can have the attributes of God. Now that our hearts are clean, we can act as priests as in Old Testament times; they acted on the behalf of others, as a mediator and an intercessor. When God is pleased with your offering, He is willing to reveal to us deep secrets, things we couldn't have known unless He reveals it to us. We become so connected to God that all we desire are the things God desires. Our will now becomes His will. God is a God of depth and once we find ourselves in His presence we will be lost in the Spirit; we will experience heights, depths and lengths we could never have imagined. We will go places in the spirit that if we should make mention of it, people would think that we are crazy. In the depths we will acquire the fruit of the Spirit, wisdom, knowledge, understanding, direction and power. Whatsoever our needs are they will be answered (1 John 5:15).

All of our needs could automatically be met without asking but God wants us to ask so that we can know that it was Him who did it and also to build our faith. We receive not because we ask not. He is waiting for us to ask so He can grant us our desires. He has already established many covenants with us in His Word. He cannot go back on His promises (Gal. 3:29). We need to know our inheritance and claim it with our legal rights from the Word of God. God has mercy on the just and on the unjust, however, only the just have legal rights through Christ to claim anything. Asking alone is not sufficient. When we ask we must also trust Him that He will answer. The Word of God says that if we ask believing it shall be done (Mark 11). When I ask God for some things I usually leave it for Him to deal with. When I do pray again, if I don't receive it, I just thank Him for what He already done since He said to pray without ceasing. God told us in 1 Peter 5 to cast all our cares upon Him because He cares for us. When we cast it on Him we are saying we have thrown it into the sea of forgetfulness. How do I know I've really cast it on the Lord? I experience a peace that is not of this world. I learn to stand still and see the salvation of the Lord. My entire life is a demonstration of living by faith. Many times I don't know how; I see no way out, but God comes through for me. I've proven time and time again that God does answer prayer once we take the necessary steps.

Faith is very good; however, having faith without knowing the Word is dangerous. I felt the desire very strongly to preach the Gospel but didn't know how that would happen because I didn't see any opportunity at the time. I acted upon faith and prayed to God to help me. How does my faith interpret the Word of God that says faith comes by hearing the Word of God (Rom. 10:17)? I also need to know that faith to preach the gospel is not enough in itself. I need to know the Word so that I can preach effectively, as the Word of God says, "study to show yourself approved…" (2 Tim.2:15). It also says we perish for lack of knowledge. (Hosea 4:6). I am not yet equipped and if I don't know the Word, the enemy can steal it out of my heart. He will tell me that God didn't call me to preach, I am just picking the call up myself. If the Word is in me, I can counteract him by letting him know that I can do all things through Christ who strengthens me (Phil. 4:13), and that all knowledge comes from the all-knowing God. God also instructed all believers to go and preach the Gospel in all the earth (Mark 16:15). This doesn't mean I have to preach in a church pulpit; if I have the Word in me, I can preach anywhere - even to my household. When it comes to the secular world, we can have whatever we want if we work hard for it. I remember in college that many of the exams were challenging, but by hard studying and perseverance I passed with flying colours. It is God's intention for us to replenish the earth but we just can't sit by complacently and expect everything to come to us. We have to go and work. Faith without works is dead according to the Word of God (James 2:20). God's promise is sure; however, in all cases we must act upon them by faith and seal them with hope. I needed money to complete my Bible course and for a year I hoped that some day God would make a way. I not only just hoped, but I also moved out in faith by writing a cheque, believing that by the time it reached the school, God would put the money in the bank. To add to my faith, I knew it would not be marked as NSF (not sufficient funds), because in the meantime I would seek and knock, knowing the door would open because it was in the will of God.

If we are not in the Spirit it is very hard to identify a powerful Christian because the definition for a powerful Christian has changed over the years. Many people identify a powerful Christian because he or she is very loud, speaks in many tongues, and knows how to memorize the Word. We could describe them as Pharisees. Another group might claim someone is powerful because he or she is a prophet, a healer, or a magic worker, but are deluded and deceived, having some other spirit behind them. However, if you show me a powerful Christian, I know that he or she is a praying Christian who doesn't just learn about it but is practicing their faith through Christ and getting permanent result.

Satan knows the promise of the Scriptures and the power of prayer; therefore, he is working very hard to stop us from praying. We must identify the things that stop us from praying because anything that stops us from being a committed, praying Christian is not from God. Christ has instructed us to pray. Prayer is the greater opportunity and privilege given to us. The Word of God is the greatest tool we need to aid us in prayer. Rom.10:17 says, "Faith comes by hearing, and hearing by the Word of God." The Word is alive, and when it is activated with faith, it not only produces results through prayer but also in our hearts. As I mentioned previously, the enemy is quite aware because this truth is a threat to him. This is why when we read the Word he comes and steals it away (Matt. 13:19). We need to fix our hearts and keep them focused on God at all times so that the Word can be hidden in it. If we truly hide it in our hearts, it is hard to come out. Like the Holy Spirit that is attached to us, so the Word can be attached once we allow it. To do this, we need to commit ourselves, and be aware of the enemy's devices as we resist him. The enemy is very cunning, but if we meditate on the Word and memorize it at all times- even in our daily chores - it is hard for the enemy to tempt us and win. Studying is so important, but even more important when it is applied to our lives. I've heard for all my life that faith without works is dead (James 2:20). I really thought I understood it until a few years back. Sometimes I have indeed moved out in faith while sometimes I sat "hoping for," believing that if God promised it, it would come to pass. After reading Dr. Myles Munroe's book "Understanding the Purpose and Power of Prayer," I realized that I wasn't always applying faith but hope and this is why it was taking so long to manifest. The book does explain that it is okay to hope for future things but a thing that is needed immediately is different.

Many Christian have spent ample time in prayer. There have even been times when it seems as if the walls of the building are coming down as a result of the shouting, screaming, crying, speaking in tongues and emotions. This can be a revolving cycle for years and years without any results. When we understand the principles of prayer, we will know that it is not the shouting, screaming, crying, speaking in tongues, emotions, or even our opinions and desires that cause prayer to be answered but by understanding and using the Word of God. Speaking the Word was the secret to the creation of the universe by God. Therefore, we too must apply the secret (power) to our prayer (the Word) and receive mighty results also.

When we use the Word in our prayers, we are asking God to intervene for us by fulfilling His purpose. The Word tells us that it is God's purpose for us to have dominion over the world. However, this cannot be done by us alone as we are finite. This is why we are not dependent on ourselves but on God through our connection with Him. We need God's Word which is alive. There is power in His Word because the Word is God who became flesh and dwelled among us (John 1:14). We need to use the Word knowing that it never fails and it will not return to God void but must accomplish everything that it sets out to do (Isa 55:11).

When prayer is done along with fasting it produces better results when it is done in accordance with righteousness. Fasting can be more effective with prayer because fasting focuses on seeking only God's interests. It might be hard to go into depth with God with only prayer, but fasting will prepare the way. In these depths, we will become unselfish and not only have the desire and interest for our own selves but also for others. Fasting causes us to be conscious of ridding our minds of everything to come into unity with God. Throughout the Bible we learn of many different situations that could only be accomplished through prayer and fasting. This is because our spiritual capacity increases during fasting. Our spiritual hearing becomes more alert; the anointing is stirred up producing supernatural power. Faith in God will also increase to believe and do the impossible. Much deliverance in the Bible was a result of fasting (Mark 9:28-29; Matthew 17:14-21). Jesus Christ is our key role model who set an example through fasting for us to follow.

Although Jesus walked the earth, He was not an ordinary man. He was God in the flesh (1 Tim 3:16). If we understood this concept we would use His name with authority. Many use the name of Jesus in their prayers and do not understand His name. This is the reason their prayer is of no effect. The name of Jesus is only effective when we understand the authority behind the power of Jesus' name. Jesus is the "Word," therefore if we understand and believe the Word we can apply it to our prayers and it will be done for us. The Word is real, it is alive and active (Heb. 4:12). The Bible tells us that all our legal authority is locked up in the name of Jesus. It is through the name of Jesus we are authorized to channel anything in the spiritual, whether in Heaven or on earth or under the earth. God only reacts to our prayer through Jesus Christ. The Bible tells us that Christ is the only mediator between man and God. It is also through the name of Jesus that man will bow powerless. We are no match to the adversary, but by mentioning the name of Jesus, the enemy trembles. We do not need to fear the enemy because Jesus has already gone to hell, terrorized him and left him powerless. It is only when we understand the attributes of the name of Jesus that we realize that it is powerful. We must also realize that if we don't have the attributes of Christ, we are not authorized to use His name. In the secular world, we must have our father's DNA in order to be his legal child. Likewise, we must have Christ's DNA (His righteousness) in order to be called sons and daughters of God.

Conclusion:

Prayer is for all believers in Christ. God has established it from before the foundation of time (it is a spiritual means) so that we could come to Him like we do to our earthly fathers and get results. There are many misconceptions on how to pray; however, all that we need for prayer is in the Word of God. Prayer is not just a ritual but a reality. Among the many that find prayer to be ineffective, I beg to differ. I could write many books on the many prayers that have been answered in my life. Among the many testimonies, I will mention only one because my life is a walking testimony. My son was born ten years after the result of a tubal ligation - this is not the testimony, as that is a story in itself (doctors says he was a miracle child). The testimony is that right after he was born, he had an infection while still in the hospital that caused a kidney problem which wasn't treated properly. Months after being discharged from the hospital, he suffered much due to medical neglect and incorrect treatment. As a result, he went through four surgeries. During these four years we went through hell. The many trips to the hospital made us feel like we could move in permanently. We prayed but nothing happened. The doctors admitted before the last surgery that he looked bad and might not make it. I went to the Lord in prayer with respect and confidence and told Him that we'd had enough. Supernaturally, God moved in the Spirit and had me lay my hands on my son's belly. My hands changed from the natural, they felt like lead. I laid my lead-weighted hands on my son's belly and God did a transformation. It has been five years since then, and my son is doing fine. He was healed by the living God; prayer does work. I am a testimony that the effective, fervent prayer of a righteous man avails much.

8

Prayer Evangelism

After trying the different methods of evangelism, we discovered prayer to be the most effective. People everywhere are going through some sort of hurt or another and would accept anything that could change their situation. In the event of their situation being changed, this could result in the greatest revival that the church has ever seen. Prayer evangelism is a tool to build relationship, thus opening the door to share the Gospel. Like all other methods of evangelism, the follow up process is one of the most important elements in prayer evangelism.

Prayer opens the pathway to share the Gospel. Many people have heard the Gospel over and over and many are also hostile toward the Gospel, but on a large scale won't refuse prayer. Studies conducted by many evangelism teams prove that the prayer method of evangelism works. We personally have used this method and it was interesting to learn that people who would not stop to listen to the Gospel, would stop and accept being prayed for.

Some people view being evangelized to as someone trying to sell them something. People don't like ulterior motives. They like things that have no strings attached to it. They certainly don't want to be tricked into going to a building to be brainwashed into giving money that they don't have. At least that's what most unbelievers think the church is doing. With all of life's pressures, they just need someone who cares. Prayer presents what they are looking for. Praying for someone is personal, relational and sincere. What an opportunity to extend the real Gospel (love)!

The praying method of evangelism is quite simple - you can use it wherever people are hurting. The doors in your neighborhood are a good place to start. All you have to do is knock on someone's door and let them know that you are in the neighborhood from (insert your church's name here), praying for people and you were wondering if there was anything they would like you to pray for. If they say "No", ask them if there is anyone in the family or anyone they know who needs prayer. Trust me! There will be someone. When they say "Yes," pray on the spot, and do not try to push the Good News down their throat. Only present the Gospel at this time if an opportunity presents itself. Before you go, thank them for allowing you to pray for them and let them know you will be praying for them regularly and you would love to follow up with them. Take their information and do not forget to follow up. This process will provide opportunities to share the Gospel. Maybe you won't preach the Gospel anytime soon from the Bible, but you may preach by your good deeds (providing help where needed). People everywhere are hurting, yet we have the solution through prayer. Jesus went everywhere healing all who were sick; it is time we stop being selfish with the power we have as believers. Let us make a change; go out and pray for those who are hurting by activating the power, faith and love that we have been given. You are capable of comforting those who are hurting, healing those who are sick. Go! You can make a difference.

If Christians were truly taking up their responsibilities and doing what the Word says, there would be great revivals. When people experience healing or become cured from their infirmities it is a natural thing to shout it out loud. Others will hear. If people were truly experiencing the power of God through a believer, news would spread abroad. While the news of reconciliation is considered foolishness to the media, the news of multiple people, from door to door, being healed of cancer, being cured of life threatening diseases, AIDS, etc. by an ordinary evangelist, is gold to newscasters. These events would hit the front page of newspapers, and be the headline news on every television station across the globe.

Approaching an individual and praying for them is best. However, it also works without you approaching them because the Lord hears the prayer of the righteous. Therefore, it is a good habit to take on the responsibility to pray for the unsaved. Prayer in evangelism also causes the unsaved to be saved without them being approached by anyone. In prayer, you can influence God and ask Him to save the unsaved. You also need to ask Him to give you strength, boldness, love and insight. Prayer brings God's plan and resources into the work of winning the unsaved. John 14:13 says, "And whatsoever ye shall ask in my name, that will I do, that the Father may be glorified in the Son." James 5:16, "Confess your faults one to another, and pray one for another, that ye may be healed. The effectual fervent prayer of a righteous man availeth much."

After we have done the first step, it is important that we do a follow up process. This process hits the nail on the head. Through the follow up, you can melt their hearts to come into the fold of Christ. Some elements in follow up: Give the person a call and offer support. This should be on a regular basis. Always take the time to listen to the person who is speaking to you. Show respect and love, and be patient. Be enthusiastic, friendly, and encouraging. Be sensitive not to ask the wrong question or say the wrong thing that will turn them off. After you get to know them a bit more, offer to meet with them. Always look for opportunities to share the Gospel. This could be few little words like "Jesus loves you." Those words might appear simple but they are huge words, especially to the hurting. Be sensitive, never over do sharing the Gospel or over stay your time. Opportunities will arise when you can share your testimony. By all means, testify! You will be surprised how your testimony could melt their hearts. Never push them to come to your church because you don't want them to get the wrong impression that you are only interested in them attending your church. If the time is right, please go ahead and invite them to church, but don't leave them isolated. Introduce them to others, especially the pastor, and make sure you take care of them while they are in your care. Also, make sure they reach home safely and continue the process until the mission is accomplished.

Prayer will ignite revival

Prayer will ignite revival as mentioned above. When people are being prayed for, they get their healing and they spread it. It has been recorded over the centuries that prayer caused many great revivals. This pattern is seen not only throughout history but also through Scriptures. In Scripture when God's people cried out in prayer because they were being judged for their sins, God responded by sending them revival. The prophets in the Old Testament also cried out on behalf of the people and God answered with revival. The New Testament records the disciples going door to door, near and far, as they prayed and multitudes were delivered. The First and Second Great Awakenings, the Laymen's Prayer Movement, and the Welsh Revival were all a result of prayer. Today we only hear of a few little revivals here and there. Why? It is simply because we are not really praying. Let's imitate the past trends and revive our nation.

9

PROPER COVERING IS NEEDED IN EVANGELIZING

Christians are special targets for the enemy; therefore, they must be protected spiritually from head to foot at all times, especially when going out into the enemy's territory. We are facing a war zone of principalities, powers, the rulers of the darkness of this world, spiritual wickedness in high places (Eph 6:12). If we are not prepared, we become prey for the enemy. I urge all those who are going out to evangelize to be fully prepared or else great consequences will result.

Some Christians are so spiritually brainless. They go out onto the battlefield partly and even at times completely defenseless; no wonder they are so beaten up…they are very lucky that they are not already dead. What a shame! They show that the soldiers in physical warfare are more sensible. Can you show me what soldier would go out onto the battlefield not fully prepared? Maybe those who have lost their minds! Why do people allow themselves to be at such immense risk? Don't they know that once they are in this world they are stepping into Satan's kingdom? God cautioned us about this war zone; He even provided us with covering and armor to protect and equip us with power for spiritual warfare.

If we use the armor God provides for us effectively, not a single one of Satan's evil arrows will get through. We must put on every item properly and also know how to use our divine weapons. This war will only be victorious in the power and might of the Lord.

The complete protection that we need is the whole armor of God.

We were first told to gird ourselves with the Belt of Truth

It is quite strange that God would tell us to put on our belt before the rest of the war garments. In the physical realm, we usually put on a belt after all of our clothing is on, but we are not dressing for a physical war zone. This is a supernatural war zone and things are very different there. I am not talking about heaven. I am referring to right here on earth. We are currently living in the physical realm, while there is a spiritual realm around us. When we go into this realm, it is very important that we have the right foundation. We MUST learn the truth and then know how to bind ourselves with this truth. This piece of armor fastens all other parts of the armor securely together. Without it the other garments won't stay intact properly. The many different cults, religions, and even those who profess Christianity will twist the truth. If we don't know the truth, we will be fooled, twisted, and even convert to their beliefs or become confused. Even the real hope that we have will be lost; we won't even believe that we have been declared righteous, we will stop trusting the Word, our faith will be damaged, we will have no peace, and our relationship with God will change.

Breastplate of Righteousness

This piece of armor is a protection for our heart, and only those who are clean can wear it. Jesus will never put Himself into a dirty vessel. Righteousness covers and protects the Word of God in our hearts. The breastplate represents Christ's righteousness in us. We are declared righteous by the grace of God; however, we are required to maintain this righteousness. How do we do this? We do this by watching what we say, what we see, what we do, our thinking, and where we go; everything should be Christ-based. If our hearts are kept pure and we are living a righteous lifestyle, Satan won't be able to touch us. If we are not covered with righteousness, Satan will search you out and know that you are powerless. He will ask you like he did in the Scripture: "And the evil spirit answered and said, Jesus I know, and Paul I know; but who are ye?" (Act 19:15).

Righteousness Maintenance Tips:

1. Consult with the maintenance manual (the Bible) before, during and after conducting service—Guidelines for maintaining righteousness can be found starting in the book of Genesis all the way to the end of Revelation.

2. Perform a spiritual body wash in prayer and fasting on a regular basis—The Holy Spirit will perform the work for you.
3. Disinfect from your head to your feet with the Holy Spirit at all times—The Holy Spirit dwells in the midst of sincere praise—therefore it is a good habit to practice praise and worship.
4. Spirit proof yourself from every corrosion (sin).
5. Perform a diagnostic check of yourself regularly in the Word.
6. Attend the congregation that is in alignment with the Word of God.

Our feet are shod with the Preparation of the Gospel of Peace

This piece is used to set people free from sin. It is having the willingness to go with the good news of salvation, wherever and whenever God leads us to go. This piece of armor will free the people from the bondage that Satan has them in.

We need our Shield of Faith to protect us

"Above all, taking the shield of faith, wherewith ye shall be able to quench all the fiery darts of the wicked" (Eph 6:16). When the enemy comes in like a flood into our lives we must have the faith to stand firmly on all of God's promises, believing that God is faithful and true to keep them. We might have the Word but without faith it won't work. The Word is the weapon and faith pulls the trigger. How do we acquire this faith? We acquire it by hearing the Word of God. The Bible says faith comes by hearing and hearing by the Word of God.

The Helmet of Salvation guards our minds

Many Christian don't realize that their mind is the battlefield for the enemy. This is the main target of the enemy. It is the place where Satan concentrates most of his attacks. This is where our spiritual warfare takes place. Satan uses our minds to distract us with carnal interests, the lust of the flesh, the lust of the eyes, and the pride of life. Satan is always persuading us to sin, and because we were once slaves to sin, we are vulnerable. Now that we have salvation, we are free from sin; we are no longer slaves and therefore do not have to yield to Satan's tricks. Through it all, God is able to keep us in perfect peace, but our minds must be stayed on Him. When our minds are on Him we will have the mind of Christ which will enable us to resist and combat the enemy.

The Sword of the Spirit - the Word of God

Again, we are fighting a spiritual war and we are no match for the enemy. He will tear us to shreds. We need a weapon and this weapon cannot be any little weapon. It cannot be the most powerful weapon on this planet. This weapon is like no other; it is the unadulterated Word of God that is sharper than any double-edged sword, penetrating even to the point of dividing soul and spirit, joints and marrow…(Hebrews 4:12). This is the main offensive weapon we have in our collection: no other weapon can match it. The enemy will flee seven ways, confused at its very presence. This weapon is so powerful that it will cut through Satan's strategies and deceits. We have the most powerful weapon of all times, the Word of God. Out of it comes unlimited weaponry for every kind of war, in this world and in the spiritual realm. This weapon is fully equipped; it even has an advanced scope that can peer down into the deepest part of hell to see what trick Satan is planning. After this insight, we can stay right here on earth and fire a Holy Ghost missile or a spiritual laser beam right down into hell. Jesus accomplished this while He was on earth. One example was when He sent the word all the way to the Centurion's home and healed the sick servant. If we have enough faith, we do not have to necessarily be present, all we have to do is send the spiritual nuclear bomb (the Word) into the prison, the hospital, oversees, etc. The Word is so powerful that it will go to hell (the root of the cause) and then travel through the arteries of the spiritual world, to the individual, and complete the needed work.

Pray in the Spirit

The final piece of the armor is prayer. We need to pray! Pray, pray and pray. Prayer in the Spirit happens when we allow our mind and spirit to maintain open conversation with God through the Holy Spirit. We are no longer praying in the flesh, but allowing the Spirit to pray through us. While we are praying, we are getting a spiritual injection to immunize us against the enemy's plots. This type of prayer is very effective in spiritual warfare because we are spiritually limited and God is able to see and attack all things for us. We sometimes don't know what has happened in the spirit, but major damage has taken place. Do you know that many things are broken down and created in the spiritual realm when we pray in the

Spirit? I have seen this happen many times. One experience I had happened while driving on the highway. God brought an elder to my mind. I started praying in the Spirit not knowing what I was praying about. A couple of days later, I saw the elder and told him about the experience I had. He was so astonished because he had been in a situation for years at his workplace which had refused to compensate him the money he was justly due. He told me that my prayer caused the funds to be released and he received the money. Another time, I was praying in the Spirit with my husband. My husband, who sees open visions frequently, told me that while I was praying he saw heaven opened and a very bright light shone down through our roof and billions of angels in white apparel stood around our entire living room, holding their swords. He said he was in awe experiencing such a sight; he even said that if he was not yet saved, that experience would have caused him to accept Christ because it was so real.

If you are not equipped and anointed by God to invade and conquer some territory, stay put for your own good. There are devils and demons waiting in line to have a field day with you. However, if you are confident that you are well covered, by all means go to whatever territory God leads you. Please note that all believers, not those who call themselves "Christians," but the true born again believers, are armed and very dangerous and are able to terrorize Satan and his kingdom. Just the other day, I was watching a television broadcast with an evangelist who was in Africa. He said while doing an open air crusade, a witch doctor come into the meeting to destroy him, and while this witch doctor was talking, the evangelist felt the power of the Holy Spirit overtake him. Immediately, this witch doctor that had started to conduct his spell began having an asthma attack and had to run for his life. This evangelist did not have to do anything because the power of God was fighting for him. This is the power we have as believers. All we need to do is stay true and God will lift up a standard for us.

Let us go and fight the good fight of faith knowing that although we are flesh and blood, we have weapons of mass destruction (the Word of God and prayer) to wipe out the enemy's army. 2 Corinthian 10:4-5 states, "For the weapons of our warfare are not carnal, but mighty through God to the pulling down of strong holds; Casting down imaginations, and every high thing that exalteth itself against the knowledge of God, and bringing into captivity every thought to the obedience of Christ."

10

DO AND DON'TS IN EVANGELISM

Do:
1. Pray before, during, and after
2. Carry your Bible and literary materials - tracts, evangelism cards, book marks, Bibles, CDs, etc.—read and know what you are handing out
3. Use simple words, no "Christianese". Keep things simple
4. Memorize key Scripture verses and use them at the appropriate time
5. Be pleasant; it is a good practice to smile while handing out materials
6. Show love and compassion
7. Allow the Holy Spirit to guide you in saying and doing the right thing
8. Evangelize to please God
9. Dress appropriately; remember you are representatives of the King of kings; you are royalty, dress modestly, be well groomed and use proper gestures
10. Be professional
11. Be patient, humble, gentle, and be a good listener
12. Answer questions, but think before you answer
13. Take the time to share the salvation message if the opportunity presents itself
14. Share your testimony—this usually works well, it can often help you to relate with the individual
15. Bring the individual, if possible to a decision point
16. Encourage the person to study the Scriptures and pray

17. Exchange follow up contact information—phone number
18. Ask questions
19. Speak clearly
20. Admit that you are a sinner too, but have been saved by grace
21. Be honest; it is okay to say you don't know when you don't have an answer

Don't:
1. Don't go out alone
2. Don't be pushy
3. Don't be like a sales person
4. Don't come on too strong
5. Don't lose patience
6. Don't get side-tracked
7. Don't be regimental, especially with the Gospel
8. Don't be too religious
9. Don't speak too fast
10. Do not touch unless it is absolutely necessary
11. Do not get caught up in useless debates
12. Do not expect people to accept you or your message
13. Do not get caught up into temptation
14. Do not present yourself as better than others
15. Do not bring pride and prejudice with you, it has no place in evangelism
16. Do not give out literature/material you do not agree with
17. When going door-to-door, do not walk on people's lawns
18. Do not stand looking through the windows
19. Do not speak to children if parents are not there. Do not litter

11

EVANGELISM GOD'S WAY

The church today has changed God's way of evangelizing. Factors that have contributed to this change are the decline in ethics, ecumenicism, moral deterioration, and human authority. There are also political, social, and economic factors. With contemporary ways of evangelizing, we miss the true benefits. Many of the methods of evangelism are geared to dealing with people's passions, feelings etc. In some sense, that is okay, but the real issue that needs to addressed in evangelism is humanity's eternal need. 1 Timothy 1: 15 reminds us: "Christ Jesus came into the world to save sinners; of whom I am chief." To understand evangelism God's way, we need to go back to basics, to the Scriptures.

The song writer wrote, *"Give me that old time religion."* Today it is so needed in our society. When comparing the church in the Scriptures with the church today, it is completely different. The church has adapted to secularism and thinks every thing is okay. One way they have justified it, is that we are living in a different dispensation and we have to change with the times. We use certain contemporary songs; water down the preaching and evangelism styles, thinking it will attract the unsaved. We have gotten so used to it that we ourselves have adopted the same habits. I do believe the churches have become too accustomed to the world's lifestyle.

We have forgotten how to completely rely on God and the Word and have become so dependent on our government and technology. A decline in ethics is also a result of adapting to worldly ethics. In worldly ethics, we see that bad is just as acceptable as good. One of the reasons we adapt, is because we are so caught up in satisfying our own personal needs. This causes us to be preoccupied and according to society, that is quite fine. The government is so much in support of our compromised ethical lifestyle, that they are willing to raise our children for us. The government in

Canada has spent millions of dollars to provide all day child care so parents can go to work. The Lord's Prayer has been out of the public school for over 20 years here in Canada. This was not God's intention. No wonder why most of our children are the way they are today. Yet we blame it on God. Most of our time is spent serving our employers, working to live in a big house, driving the best cars…this leaves us with no time to spend with our children, with God or doing the things of God. We have become like robots, with society dictating to us what we are to do, and like zombies, we comply, even if it means that we must compromise.

The church today is caught up in using contemporary evangelism to accomplish what Jesus commissioned us to do. This method is very convenient, but not very effective. Census data confirms that only a few unbelievers are coming to Christ through the works of evangelism. If we are to fulfill the Great Commission, we must follow the steps Jesus instructed us, in its entirety. Nothing else will do.

While Jesus was on earth, he demonstrated evangelism. First, He lived a life to please his Father. Our first priority should be to please God. If we do so, everything else will fall into place. Jesus could have just come to earth and died, but He demonstrated evangelism for our learning. If we go back to Scripture and observe everything that Jesus did, we would be very effective in evangelism. It is very good to take note of how much time Jesus dedicated in His life to prayer. He spent much time in prayer and was very effective in His exploits. Prayer is an important key to evangelism. Without prayer we are on our way to failure. We also read in Scriptures that everywhere Jesus went, He did good, He healed the sick, raised the dead, and cast out demons. Jesus developed relationships; He spent time and was sacrificial: those that evangelize should exhibit Christ-like characteristics. People everywhere are in despair. If we were doing what Jesus did, we would see people from all walks of life coming to the truth. If Christ is being lifted up, He will draw all men unto himself. Jesus told us to teach everything he taught in the Gospels, including healing the sick, with signs and wonders following the believers. All power and authority was given to us. What is the use of this power and authority if it is not being used? Spiritual gifts are not for personal gain, but to build up the church. Matthew 10:7 says, "And as ye go, preach, saying, The kingdom of heaven is at hand. Heal the sick, cleanse the lepers, raise the dead, cast out devils: freely ye have received, freely give."

With all that Jesus did, He did not fail to proclaim repentance (Matthew 4:17). People will come as a result of the sovereign God being glorified; but for them to be truly saved, they need to understand that they must repent. Many people come to the church because their physical needs are met and do not truly understand that they must repent. I attended a church for a few years and repentance was never preached. When asked, I was told that "it is not necessary, it is negative, and God's love is sufficient to save". This is why you find many that are religious but lost within the walls of the church.

Evangelism in scriptures

Jesus conducted much personal evangelism. In Jesus' personal evangelism, he did not throw the Gospel at anyone. In most instances, He listened and waited for an opportunity to respond. John the Baptist and Peter conducted mass evangelism, Paul used dialogue evangelism (Acts 17:16-34). The early church in Act 5:42 practiced visitation evangelism. The Scriptures say that they went from house to house. All these methods of evangelism are great; however, they will be ineffective without certain principles: love, compassion, understanding, discernment, patience, the preaching of the Gospel and prayer.

The first principle that we need to exhibit is love. Everything else will follow. It makes no sense to go out trying to love the unsaved when we fall short of love in our local congregations. If we do not practice love towards our Christians family, what makes us think that we will practice it toward the unsaved? We need to practice at home before we go abroad. Do we love those who are in our church? When I talk about love, I am not talking about the love everyone is using in vain, or Hollywood love, but the real love that: "suffereth long, and is kind; charity envieth not; charity vaunteth not itself, is not puffed up, doth not behave itself unseemly, seeketh not her own, is not easily provoked, thinketh no evil; Rejoiceth not in iniquity, but rejoiceth in the truth; Beareth all things, believeth all things, hopeth all things, endureth all things." (1 Cor. 13: 4-7). I am also talking about the love that loves our neighbors as ourselves. Can we really live up to this love? We should, but unfortunately, we have fallen short. No wonder we don't see great revivals across the globe. If we don't have true love, how are we going to bring others into our church? The church is messed up enough and needs to bring back love within the walls so people will feel loved when they come to visit. Also, if there is love among us, others will automatically want to go and share it. If we love those who are in the body of Christ, the Gospel will be preached. If we evangelize with real love, others will come to the Lord as a result.

Simple Steps to provide a loving environment:
- First, we need to search ourselves and see where we fall short
- Admit our shortcomings
- Ask God to forgive us, to lead us into love and to endue us with His agape love
- Abide in God, spend ample time with God, read the Word with understanding, and read it regularly
- Detach yourself from unloving Christians and seek to associate yourselves with those who exhibit love
- Try to build relationships with those in your church, get to know their names (people feel special when you know their name)
- Let someone know that you are praying for them and you should be truly praying for them
- Demonstrate hospitality towards those in your church
- Invite other Christians to your home, learn their birthdates, and express love to them by giving them a gift
- Make it your duty to visit and extend love and compassion to other Christians in their time of need
- Visit them when they are sick; at home, or in the hospital
- Call those that you do not see in church
- Seek to know the needs within your church and meet them

I do not discredit tracts, but in the Scriptures, Jesus certainly did not give out tracts to evangelize people with the Gospel. Today we use encounter evangelism (a microwave method) but Jesus used process evangelism (the slow cooker method). In the story of the woman at the well, *Jesus traveled through Samaria.* Sometimes we should just go for a stroll and let an opportunity present itself. *Jesus came to Jacob's well; He was tired and so He sat down by the well.* The mall is a good place to look for opportunities. It could be our well since those days were different from today. "*When a Samaritan woman came to draw water, Jesus said to her,*

"Will you give me a drink?" Today if we ask someone for a drink it could be a bit awkward but we can ask other questions that could start a conversation. The Samaritan woman said to him, "How is it that thou, being a Jew, askest drink of me, which am a woman of Samaria? for the Jews have no dealings with the Samaritans." Nevertheless, Jesus associated with her. Sometimes those we come in contact with will have been dishonored by others and are unapproachable, yet we need to treat them with love as you would with anyone else. Jesus' evangelism method started out with a simple conversation and ended with someone accepting salvation. The early church followed God's way of evangelism. They were more informal = fellowship. Today's church is very formal = program. The secret to evangelism is discipleship: the best way to win souls is to love people.

Evangelism should not be only within the walls of our churches; neither should it be mistaken for giving out a few tracts or knocking on doors. Jesus not only preached in the synagogues, but also spoken to people wherever they were. He met the Samaritan woman at the well, the disciples at the sea shore, ministered to a demon possessed man in a graveyard, spoke to Zacchaeus up in a sycamore tree, and went into villages and towns to minister, as well as in the market places, and in people's own homes and streets. Jesus told us to go into the world to meet people.

He did not invite them to come to His church. Do not try too hard to get the people to your church; the church is messed up enough and is in need of help too. Invite people to the Lord only. Forget about your own gratification. Our aim should not be for the growth of the church directory.

12

STYLES OF EVANGELISM

Matthew 20:19 and Eph. 6:19 tell us that all are called to evangelize. Therefore, it's not whether we evangelize or not, I believe the problem is HOW? The way we evangelize should be determined by our personalities. Not every one has the same personality and not one style of evangelism fits every situation. Let's look at some different styles of evangelism and determine what style fits you.

Incarnational

This one is mandatory for every Christian. To be incarnate, means that you are no longer living in the flesh. You are now living in newness of life by the Spirit of God. Therefore, you are now to live the Gospel. You need to let your light shine Matthew 5:16. We must live God's way so that when we do speak, it is genuine.

Invitational

To invite someone is so easy—all you have to do is ask. They will either answer "yes" or "no." Sometimes they will say "no," but really mean "yes." Don't be afraid to ask them again. When you least expect it, they will say "okay!"

Testimonial

Everyone has a testimony or story of how Jesus has changed their life. Share it whenever you can. You might just amaze yourself when you see the impact it could have on someone who is without hope. Your testimony was not meant to be kept to yourself; it is meant to be shared.

In John 9, the blind man who was healed by Jesus refuses to argue with the authorities as to whether Jesus was a good man or bad. "All I know is this," he says. "I was blind, and now I can see." We too, have personal experiences with Jesus to share just like this blind man.

Compassion

This style speaks volumes to people and is so effective. Those single mothers that come to your church are hoping for a little compassion. The bereaved would be comforted; the homeless and orphans will find a home and a family. What about the unsaved?

Get involved in some kind of compassionate evangelism. People in desperate situations can't wait to hear you share and give them some hope. It is not hard to do. In some cases, all you might need to do is take the time to listen to someone. Giving someone a card with a word of encouragement along with a little token, works well for any need. Someone might mention that they have nothing in their cupboard. Don't only say you will pray for them; if you can help, fill that cupboard.

Confrontational

This style can be very aggressive. It is a direct, in your face approach, requiring boldness. This style can be abrupt, loud, and bold. Many people are too shy to share the Gospel and would be afraid to use this style. This style is used in Scriptures. For example, in Acts 2:22-41, Peter used it when he was preaching to the crowd at Pentecost. When they asked him what must they do to be saved, he did not beat around the bush, but boldly told them to "REPENT." He was not shy about it because he was confident in the Word of God.

Intellectual

This style is used by those who are scholars, who are well-versed intellectually. They are able to present a rational case and debate with other intellectuals. The Apostle Paul was well known for this style. He preached to philosophers (Acts 17:15-34).

Relational (also known as friendship evangelism)

This style is probably the easiest for us to use. Levi (Matthew) in Luke 5, invited fellow tax collectors to his home: His idea was to throw a feast, and invite the tax collectors over. He was setting up the tax collectors to meet Jesus. Instead of trying to get people to your church immediately, it is best to try this approach so that you can build closeness with them, build a relationship first, and then invite them to church.

Hospitality/Serving

A dinner is a good way to relax people and create trust. Dorcas is described in Acts 9 as hospitable. She expressed acts of kindness and charity. This style will demonstrate love. It will touch one's heart.

The Supernatural Style

Allow God to minister through you. Sometimes the Holy Spirit will give you a word of knowledge for some one. Often the person will be amazed because no one else knew what God had revealed except the person.

The Love Style

John 4:7: "Beloved, let us love one another…" How does it work? How do I use it to benefit others? You just love! Love is a powerful weapon, it is one of the most powerful weapons on earth… love conquers a multitude of sins. God's love will seek out the needy, the hurting, and the lonely. If you have God's love, you will be an instrument of love. Love must be active at all times. It is the greatest weapon to win the unsaved. This love has conquered the world. It is the love of God that is going to be poured out in the last days. This love manifests itself in us. His love goes way behind our little problems. His love will overtake us. His great love is the greatest weapon against hate/rage. God's desire is to put that love in us as an expression of God. He poured it into our lives so that we can give it to this dry, thirsty land (thirsty people) which will spring forth into new life. The love of God is like the sun; it covers everything in your life. The world doesn't know how much Christ loves them. That's why they are not serving Him. The Christians are not showing love, so the unsaved don't know where to find it. The Holy Spirit will reveal love in us but He has nothing to work with. When the world sees the love of God being poured out to them they will see the love of God. How do you show love? You use your hands, your feet, and your mouth. Love even your enemy. Manifest the fruit of the Spirit. You can't fight love. You just have to accept it. It cannot be rejected, it will just keep coming. When we have the love of God, you don't only love certain people; you love everyone, even the unlovable. Go out of your way to love people. God's love goes beyond all the barriers, the hate, the…[7]

Every attack against you is an opportunity to show God's love, and God's favour.

---

[7] Dr. Rondo Thomas Teachings, Vice President of Canada Christian College

13

Example Script

For Street Evangelism, Special Event Evangelism, Neighborhood Evangelism, Work place Evangelism and Door to door evangelism, etc.

Street Evangelism

"Hi, how are you? Can we have a minute of your time to share about the love of Jesus?" Refer to the salvation message.

Special Event Evangelism

"We would like to invite you to a (special event) on (date). Do you think you can make it?" Provide them with an event flyer, etc.

Neighborhood Evangelism

"We are a new church in the area. Can we ask you several short questions?" or, "Good morning/afternoon, we are from _____Church, just around the corner and we are inviting the neighborhood to come out and join us for our afternoon service (concert, youth service, convention etc.)." Give them a flyer, order of service, etc. and/or a tract.

Work Place Evangelism

- The simplest evangelism is to allow the light of Christ to shine through you. Matthew 5:14-16 says, "Ye are the light of the world. A city that is set on a hill cannot be hid. Neither do men light a candle, and put it under a bushel, but on a candlestick; and it giveth light unto all that are in the house. Let your light so shine before men, that they may see your good works, and glorify your Father which is in heaven."

- You should always strive to be moral, courteous and blameless.
- Don't participate in events that are beyond good moral character.
- Be aware of other coworker's needs and conditions and develop relationships with them so that you can provide help, prayer and/or refer them to resources that can help them.
- Always carry literature on you so that if an opportunity arises, you can provide them with tracts, Bibles, etc.
- When opposition arises, respond in love. Do not retaliate but do good to those who mistreat and hurt you. It is hard, but turn the other cheek. Always exhibit the fruits of the Spirit.

Door-to-Door Evangelism
- Ring the doorbell once, and if you do not hear it, you may wish to knock.
- Stand where they will see you when the door opens (hinge side), as well as when they look through the peep hole in the door.
- Again, you can use the same generic questions as above: "Hi, how are you, Can we have a minute of your time to share about the love of Jesus?" Refer to the salvation message.
- Have a Gospel pamphlet available in your hand to leave with a person who is not interested.
- One person should be designated to do the speaking prior to arriving at the door, the other should pray.
- The experienced person should begin, and after several houses, the less experienced one can give it a try.
- If you are in a mixed pair, the female could speak to women and the male to men.
- Leave literature when there is no answer. Place it in a safe but visible place on the screen door.
- It is a good practice not to walk across people's lawns; do not speak to children (even teens) if parents are not present, don't make a lot of noise on people's property, do not litter, and don't peep into windows or go to the back of the house.

Another method you can use when going **door to door**: when someone opens the door, say "good morning" or "good afternoon." "My Name is _____from _____ Church and we are in the neighborhood praying for people. Is there anything you would like us to pray for?" If they say no, ask them if they are sure. If they persist on saying 'no' leave a tract and thank them for their time.

Preparing for the Gospel

Diagnosis: "The first task of the physician is to correctly diagnosis the case, or his prescription will be at random.

So with the soul-physician. The doctor asks questions so couched as to reveal the inward condition, and the doctor of souls must do the same.

The questions at first may be general, but must proceed to the particular."

[8]Begin with a generic question (as above), then use assurance. *"If you were to die today do you know if you would go to heaven?"* They may respond as follows:

"Well, I go to church."
"I am a good person."
"I hope so."
"I don't know."

You can respond by saying: It is very good to attend church but that won't get you to heaven. The only way you can go to heaven is if you repent from your sins, believe that the Lord Jesus Christ died for your sins and accept Him into your heart.

Being good is a good thing, but we are not saved by works but through grace. The Bible says, "For by grace are ye saved through faith; and that not of yourselves: it is the gift of God" (Ephesians 2:8). Salvation is a gift from God. Jesus is that free gift and you just receive Him by faith. You can know for sure that you will go to heaven by receiving Him."

Sharing the Gospel can be simple, but you must familiarize yourself with it before going out. Always take your Bible with you so you can refer to it. You can also refer to a Gospel tract. Most tracts are designed with the appropriate Gospel message that the unsaved need to hear. You might

---

8 www.baptistbiblebelievers.com

only need to share your testimony and that is fine. Testimonies are usually effective. However, before bringing the unsaved to a decision point, the Gospel must be explained which includes: Man's sinful state (Romans 3:23), men are accountable for their sins (Romans 6:23), Christ paid the penalty (Romans 5:8), it is not by works any one is saved, and there is an urgency to receiving Christ (2 Corinthians 6:1-2).

Bringing to a point of decision: This is the time you would lead them into the sinner's prayer. Before you do so, please make certain that they understand their position and the requirement to be saved. After they have prayed the sinner's prayer, at the end of the conversation pray for them and confirm their prayer for salvation over them, pray for their covering, and their new walk.

"The Sinners Prayer"

Heavenly Father! I ask that you forgive me of my Sins. I confess with my mouth and believe with my heart that Jesus is your Son, And that he died on the Cross that I might be forgiven and have Eternal Life. I believe that Jesus rose from the dead and I ask you right now to come in to my life and be my personal Lord and Savior. In Jesus Name I pray, Amen.

Why pray the sinner's prayer?

Romans 10 verse 9-10-13 says,

"That if thou shalt confess with thy mouth the Lord Jesus, and shalt believe in thine heart that God hath raised him from the dead, thou shalt be saved. For with the heart man believeth unto righteousness; and with the mouth confession is made unto salvation…For whosoever shall call upon the name of the Lord shall be saved."

What it is to believe

Some one once said, "I believe in CHRIST, but the devils also believe and tremble, and they are not saved."

"There are obviously two kinds of belief - one purely mental, the other involving the whole of the moral nature. The purely mental opinion that it is true that CHRIST lived and died for men, works no saving change in the heart or life. What, then, is it to believe to the salvation of your soul? It is to so put your confidence in CHRIST as being what He claimed to be your SAVIOUR and sin-bearer-that you put yourself absolutely in His hands for salvation.

'John 1:12 shows that believing and receiving are synonymous "As many as received him"-as personal SAVIOU and sin-bearer-thereby received "power to become the sons of God."

The Divine Order

The *fact*, *faith* and the *feeling*.
Jesus did it-on the cross.
God says it- in His Word.
I believe it-in my heart.

Feeling that you are saved cannot come before you are saved, any more than feeling you are well after an illness cannot come until you are well. And as you cannot be saved without believing, faith must precede feeling. As faith must have a fact to rest on, the fact must precede faith.

I believe it, not because I feel it, but because God says it and Jesus did it. Make sure that the anxious one is resting not on his own feelings but on God's Word".[9]

---

[9] www.baptistbiblebelievers.com

14

EVENT EVANGELISM

Revival and Crusades: These are often used by many popular evangelists. Yet they can be used by anyone. They are very effective when organized properly. These styles work best when you involve as many labourers as possible. What is an evangelism event without the unsaved? The labourers' responsibility is to go out and invite people, especially the unsaved. This can be neighbors, friends, family, coworkers; any one who can attend.

Street and Open Air Preaching: Jesus, John the Baptist, Peter and Paul were all Open Air Preacher. They preached the Gospel and many came to Christ as a result. This type of event can be intimidating but effective. Many churches report that many come to know Christ as a result of Open Air and Street events. So often we see the church preaching to the church, on dry ground and refusing to go into the deep sea. Street and open air evangelism is coming off of dry land and going fishing out in the deep sea. Not all countries or cities allow these events. However, they can be done regardless, just discreetly. These events have been done by our team in parts of the world that do not allow them. When our team goes out, we do not try to make a scene, but look for creative ways to preach. For example, we can stand at a street side and when someone approaches us, we can share the Gospel with them. Other people passing by will be drawn to us. Instead of preaching to one person, we now have an audience! When those that are in authority come by, the Lord will convict them too, or they can only tell you to leave. The message has been preached by this time. If it comes to the point of being thrown into jail, so what if we are put in jail for Christ? This has happened many times in the past and continues even today. Another creative way is to put a picnic together in the park, put together a gospel band, and as people pass by, share the Gospel and give out tracts, Bibles, etc.

Evangelistic Special Day Events: Friends' Day, Christmas celebrations, Thanksgiving, Halloween, Good Friday, Easter, Baby Dedications etc. these events draw crowds. You can get the entire congregation involved. Make certain you have someone write down everyone's contact information for follow up. Make sure that they are well looked after. It is a good idea to prepare a free meal, a snack and refreshments for them. Also, you can give them a little gift of appreciation. Make sure that you follow up and extend love and compassion.

Evangelism meal: this is a very good practice, especially at Thanksgiving. Invite the neighborhood, the homeless, etc. to a free dinner at your church. People love 'freebies' and it is a great way to build relationships and socialize with people.

Evangelistic Need Seminars: People are searching for different solutions but their real need is Jesus. The church can put on seminars to attract them. How about putting on a Job Fair, courses on how to fix things around the house, computer workshop, how to buy your first home, etc.? With these seminars, you can incorporate the Gospel.

Evangelism Youth Explosion Event: Get your church, especially the youth, and organize some events. For example: a gospel party where you invite other Christians and non-Christian youth. Have the band or bands play gospel music that the youth love (not the old time music), do some plays, play games, have food and drinks, etc. Make sure that the Gospel is preached sometime during the event. Do not forget to go out into the neighborhood and invite the youth. Talk to parents so that they could involve their youth. Let your youth and the entire church invite their family, friends, and any youths they know to the event. When advertising, let the youth know it is not a boring church event, but their kind of event, i.e. contemporary songs with Christian words. This is a way to get them to come. They won't come with our kind of music.

Evangelistic Drama Events: People love to be entertained. Put on a Gospel play or a non-gospel play, making sure that the Gospel is incorporated into it.

Community: Get involved in community projects

Street Work: Go out on the street and speak to people, hand out a tract or a Bible. People will notice you and even start a conversation.

15

Door to Door Evangelism and Critics

Many critics have doubted the method of door to door evangelism and one of the reasons is because they have not tried it properly, or not at all. We have become so dependent on new technologies in the efforts of evangelism and have had no time for the effective, personalized, traditional method. Many evangelists have had to challenge the critics' views. After many studies, the conclusion is that door to door evangelism is far and away one of the most effective methods. We have researched many churches in Canada and the USA and found out that door to door evangelism is an effective way to win the lost. On the other hand, the maintaining of the growth will be determined by consistent follow up which includes visitation, great resources, phone calls and hospitality.

Most studies conducted in the USA looked at more than 400 churches in their study before determining that door to door evangelism is one of the most effective methods. Other pastors looked at these studies and began to use the door to door method and have also found that it works.

Billy Graham used this method. Anyone who is accustomed to the Billy Graham Crusades will attest to the thousands who are in attendance at his meetings. From research we found out that he has a team who organized thousand of workers from many different churches who would visit thousands of homes prior to the Crusade. He also had a team in place that would effectively follow up with people after the Crusade.

According to a published report from the Council of Churches, 2008 Year Book of American and Canadian churches, the fastest growing churches in the USA and Canada were the Church of the Latter day Saint's and the Jehovah's Witness who attributed their growth to door to door evangelism.

"In 1960, D. James Kennedy graduated from seminary and began preaching at the Coral Ridge Church in Fort Lauderdale, FL. After just eight months of ministry there, the congregation dwindled from 45 to 17 believers. Although he was very discouraged about what was happening, he would not give up. He realized the problem was that he lacked courage to confront unbelievers with the truth of the gospel. To his surprise, he was invited to Decatur, GA to conduct a gospel campaign for ten days. He preached each evening, but during the mornings and afternoons, he received training and visited homes, presenting the gospel door-to-door. Those experiences at the doorways of the unsaved would transform his ministry completely. After the evangelistic campaign he returned to the Coral Ridge Church, where he implemented the principles he had learned in Georgia—he called these principles "Evangelism Explosion". By presenting unsaved men and women with the claims of the gospel on their doorsteps, the Coral Ridge Church grew from 17 individuals to over 2,000 in nine years. These simple door-to-door evangelistic principles would be the means of winning thousands to Christ in the United States and in 93 other lands throughout the world."[10]

Many Christians assume that door to door evangelism doesn't work yet have not tried it. According to research conducted by Ray Comfort it is said that 97% of "Christians" will not share their faith before they die. What a high percentage! Christians really need to wake up. Another reason why door to door evangelism isn't working is because some Christians are not trained properly and there is no follow up process in place. I have come across evangelists who are passionate about going door to door but when asked about their procedure, it was surprising to find that they are lacking the skills.

Door to door evangelism does work. As a matter of a fact, it is the original method of reaching the lost from Jesus' time. This method worked very well, it continues from the book of Acts up to today. Every church should use this method if they are serious in seeing the lost come to Christ. After all, aren't we supposed to take the Gospel to the unsaved? Even Jesus knew that this would work. This is one of the reasons He told us to "go." The unsaved won't come; we must take the Gospel to them - even to their homes. Do they live in caves? If so, then we need to go to the caves; where ever they are we should go.

---

10 D. James Kennedy, Evangelism Explosion, Wheaton, IL, Tyndale House Publishers, 1977, p6

16

TRACT & EVANGELISM TIPS

- Keep a few tracts in your 'back pocket' then slip one under you wherever you sit down. In the bus, restaurant, subway, airport etc. When you get up, the Gospel has been left for someone that God has been preparing. You can slide them under the tip at a restaurant, leave them on the washroom counter, store counters, and pin on public bulletin boards in Laundromats, apartment complexes and lunch rooms. Most of these places are designed for leaving such information.
- You can place one in the envelope when paying your bills, give as a bookmark, even quietly place in someone's shopping bag.
- It is always a good practice to carry tracts with you at all times. You don't know when you might come in contact with someone you are not able to speak with but can allow a tract to do the talking for you.
- It is a very good idea to personalize your tract with your own personal testimony so that you can say to people, "This is my own testimony." People like to relate to reality.
- Some people don't have time to stop and talk to you because of their busy schedule. While they are passing by, say "Excuse me, can I give you one of these?" They can either accept it or reject it; you don't know, just pray and leave it up to the Lord.

Evangelism Tips

1. Pray everyday that God will give you the opportunity to evangelize Also, pray before you go out for boldness and protection
2. Look for every opportunity to evangelize the Gospel

3. Look at people as Jesus sees them
4. Share from your heart with compassion
5. Be yourself—don't try to be someone else, don't try to evangelize from a script
6. Memorize their name and use it frequently when you are sharing the Gospel
7. Be friendly. Smile, be kind and express love. You are a representative of the Sovereign King
8. Keep the conversation general for a brief time—don't waste their time—get to the point of sharing the Gospel
9. Always leave a positive note - they might be rude to you - you can respond that God loves you—don't be hostile
10. Always leave a tract with a phone number on the back
11. Stay on the subject of salvation
12. Go two by two—only one should be doing the talking while the other prays
13. Always carry your New Testament with you
14. No matter how short your presentation speech is, practice it over and over again
15. Decide which person should be the spokesperson before you go
16. Ring the door bell or knock then step back
17. Never go into a home if a wife or husband is home alone
18. Don't stay too long
19. Be a good listener

17

Your Witnessing Audience

Our audience in evangelism is of course the unsaved that are all around us in the world. Although they are sinful, Jesus loves them just the same. As a matter of a fact, Jesus did not come for the righteous but for the unrighteous. Christians are no better than the unbelievers in themselves. They are substantially better off because of Jesus Christ. The only good the believer has comes from the Lord (Philippians 3:9). Psalm 14:3 says, "They are all gone aside, they are all together become filthy: there is none that doeth good, no, not one."

Witnessing audience:
1. Coworkers
2. Family members
3. Church members
4. Friends
5. Homosexuals
6. Neighbors

Co-workers—you can preach the Gospel by your works. We are interacting with different people everyday. This is a great opportunity to share Christ. How do we share Christ? Be diligent in your work, be a good steward, set a good example by your work ethic. Show respect to co-workers and employers. When there is conflict around you, respond in a Christ-like way. Show love, be calm, be forgiving, have a steadfast spirit, be friendly and courteous, and show genuine interest in your coworker's and bosses' lives. When you are aware of situations they are going through, please ask them if you can pray for them. The good impression you leave will cause people to hear and see Christ in you.

Church members—not all who go to church are redeemed. The Gospel has been preached, however, many are immune to it. In other words, the Gospel means nothing to them. In this case, it is our duty to live the Gospel so that they can be impacted by it. We should never overlook the fact that there are unbelievers who attend church for different reasons. The seed has been planted and they might be in the process of being watered, but have not yet been reaped from the spiritual harvest of Christ. It is our responsibility to ensure the process continues; therefore, we must not only sow and water, but also do what is right according to Scriptures so that Christ can draw them into His spiritual fold. 1 Peter 3:1 addresses unbelieving husbands, "…if any obey not the word, they also may without the word be won by the conversation of the wives."

Family members/ Friends— they are the hardest ones to witness to, yet they are the most convenient because they are at our fingertips. How do we witness to them? We do not have to preach a sermon to them. The best sermon is to live the Gospel so they can read the pages of Scripture by our lifestyle. You have the opportunity to shine your light bright. "Let your light so shine before men, that they may see your good works, and glorify your Father which is in heaven" (Matthew 5:16). Let them see how Jesus is working in your life. Christ in you will speak volumes; Christ in you will cause them to respond with questions. This is your opportunity to share Christ with them and don't be afraid to share your testimony at every opportunity you get, giving God the glory. If Christ is lifted up, then He will draw all men unto Himself.

Homosexuals—homosexuals should not be highlighted as different from other sinners because they are in violation of God's law just like any other sinner. Sin is sin and they too qualify for God's grace. We should not overlook them; they also need to know that they are sinners…they must also know, that such a lifestyle is sin and they can be forgiven if they turn from it. While witnessing to them, it is not wise to engage in any arguments. Your responsibility is to provide them with the Gospel, and leave God to be their judge.

Neighbors—the first thing to do is to pray for them. Always exhibit Godly conduct—1 Peter 2:12 says, "Having your conversation honest among the Gentiles: that, whereas they speak against you as evildoers, they may by your good works, which they shall behold, glorify God in the day of visitation". Good deeds are a very good witnessing tool. Offer to give them a hand in things you notice need doing around their yard, give them a gift, bake them something nice, offer them a ride if they don't have a car, etc. People notice the Gospel more through actions than through words. Be friendly, offer to look after their mail while they are on vacation, invite them over for dinner- it will open an opportunity to share the Gospel.

18

WITNESSING TO CULTS

1. Pagans & Wiccans
2. Those Involved in New Age Religion
3. Catholics
4. Jehovah's Witnesses
5. Mormons
6. Judaism
7. Universalists
8. Muslims
9. The Cult Church
10. Additional information on Cults
11. The "Jesus" of the Cults

Brief Pointers Witnessing to Pagans and Wiccans
- Remember that you are covered under the blood of Jesus Christ and nothing can harm you.
- Make sure you examine yourself to make sure there is no sin in your life.
- PRAY before going out.
- Never go out alone, bring someone that is spiritually mature enough to cover your back.
- Show them genuine Christian love, and pray for them.
- Respect their beliefs (although this does not mean you have to agree with them).

- Try and understand their beliefs. Don't just read Christian articles and books about Paganism - do the research yourself. Get some books out by respected pagan authorities, take notes from them, and share interesting portions of what you discover with them.

- Ask them what they believe about Christianity (many pagans have a distorted image of what Christianity is). Where they are wrong, correct them.

- Understand that many Pagans and Wiccans have had bad experiences with churches in one way or another. Some have even been brought up in an environment which professes Christianity.

- Stress the relationship that Christians have with Christ.

- Stress the heart of the Gospel: The death, resurrection, ascension, and second coming of Christ.

- Outline the strengths and reliability of the Bible, as many pagans reject it as unreliable.

- Understand that most Pagans and Wiccans reject the concept of objective truth. Stress the truth which is to be found in Christ."[11]

Witnessing to those Involved in New Age Religion

The New Age Religion is a cultic religion whose source is Satan. This movement has been widely spread since the 20th Century. Jesus warned us of them in Mark 13:22, "For false Christs and false prophets shall rise, and shall shew signs and wonders, to seduce, if it were possible, even the elect." Some of the New Age Religion beliefs are as follows: Belief in astrology, crystals as a source of healing or energizing power, and the practice of reading tarot cards. They also believe that God is a state of higher consciousness which man may reach. Basically, they believe that each person is God. Satan really has control of these people's minds! Romans 10:3-4 says, "For they being ignorant of God's righteousness, and going about to establish their own righteousness, have not submitted themselves unto the righteousness of God. For Christ is the end of the law for righteousness to every one that believeth."

---

[11] © Spotlight Ministries, Vincent McCann, 2002, spotlightministries.org.uk

A few points we should know in reaching them:

- As with all other encounters, we need to pray.
- Remember that you are in a spiritual war zone and need to be properly covered.
- If you are not well-versed in the Word, give them some literature and leave. Never argue about the Scripture with them because they will twist you up. They will use words from the Scriptures, but will take them out of the context of biblical meaning.
- Be knowledgeable in the Word. Look out for contradictions and use the Word of God to combat them. Remember the Word of God is powerful.
- Always show love.

Witnessing to Roman Catholics

A Method of Presenting the Truth to Seeking Catholics

Presented by Richard Bennett, Former Dominican Missionary Priest of 21 Years

I. Dealing with Various Situations

　A. Remember to present the Roman Catholic with the dilemma of our sin in the sight of the Holy God.

　　1. Use questions to get them thinking, like:

　　　a. "How can we sinners stand before the Holy God?"

　　　b. "How can you and I have eternal life?"

　　　c. "What does it mean to be born again?"

　　　d. "Why did the sinless Son of God die such a horrible death on the cross?"

　　2. Declare confidently what the Scriptures say about this dilemma according to their understanding. To do this, you must get them to <u>accept the Scriptures as truth</u>, - without the need to run to philosophers and private interpretations (2 Peter 1:20).

　B. **Dealing with the Trained Catholic** - They will usually use the following verses and suppositions:

1. <u>The need for Tradition</u> (2 Thessalonians 2:15). Present Acts 2:42 and 2 Timothy 2:2. And then take them to Revelation 22:18, 19

2. <u>The special powers of Peter</u> (Matthew 16:18, 19). Take them to Matthew 16:21-23 for the issue of Peter's supremacy, and to Matthew 18:18-20 to show that ALL the disciples had access to answered prayer. Peter was only a fellow elder and apostle. He is never mentioned as having been in Rome by Paul in the book of Romans. Even if he had been in Rome, it was only as an apostle, and not as an elder or pastor.

3. <u>More special powers of the Church</u> (Matthew 18:18). Show them the context when Jesus talks about people praying to "bind" Satan's work, and with praying that God will open people's hearts.

4. <u>The literalness of the Eucharist</u> (John 6:53-56). Take them over to John 6:63, 7:37-39, and John 10:7-9.

C. **Dealing with the Indifferent Catholic** - They just don't care about eternity

1. Use the death of Christ on the cross as the means of getting them to realize that someone died innocently as a substitute for sin. And could it have been for **their** sin?

2. Be very careful not to lord your own knowledge over them because you will put them into a defensive stance that will only work against you. Get them to battle with Christ, not with you!

3. Use questions. Be slow to give the answers, sometimes not even giving your answer at all. Allow the other person the time to think about the seriousness of the questions you are asking.

4. Use the Sword of the Spirit to cut, rather than just "nick" the heart of the indifferent. Ask, "What does the Bible mean when it says, 'The wages of sin is death?'" (Romans 6:23).

5. As they respond, direct them to the Holy God of the Bible, showing them that all of us are sinners in His sight - use Romans 3:10-ff. Show them also Isaiah 64:6!

D. **Dealing with the Self-Satisfied Catholic** - "I'm doing just fine."

   1. Show them John 14:23 where Jesus says, "If a man love me, he will keep my words..." Ask, "How can we keep His words?" Show the person Matthew 7:24-29 where Jesus compares keeping His words to building a house upon a rock, or upon sand, based on our obedience.

   2. Forget talking about your church versus their church.

   3. Be careful to only use Biblical words, and make sure that he or she understands the terms. Don't use the phrase, "have you received Christ?" They think that they literally do every time they attend Mass.

   4. Show them that no matter how good they may be, they can never be good enough (Romans 3:23), and that God had to send His Son in every person's place (John 3:16).

E. **Dealing with the Seeking or Interested Catholic** - "I am no saint!"

   1. Show them Christ crucified and ask them if He died for them, and their sins specifically (not for the sins of the world generally).

   2. Show them their inability to save themselves (Ephesians 2:1)

   3. Take them to Ephesians 2:8, 9 and show them that salvation is a free gift because of Christ (Romans 6:23-.

F. **Dealing with Confusion.** The Catholic mind-set is one of ingrained ideas handed down from generation to generation, e.g., prayers to Mary, infant baptism, what about all the heathen, etc. They all can be, and must be demolished by the Sword of the Spirit.

   1. "We Catholics have an optimistic view of Creation. We believe that God sees everything He made as very good - not evil like you people do." Show them Romans 5:12, Jeremiah 17:9, Mark 7:20-23, and Romans 3:10 and 3:23. Ask him or her what God thinks of His creation now that sin dominates!

   2. "As Catholics, we don't have blind faith. Our faith rather is based upon reason. We have always had a profound respect

for reason, and we promote understanding. St. Augustine tried to understand all of history from the perspective of Catholic faith. St. Thomas Aquinas used the best of medieval science found in Aristotle. We Catholics are open to all human knowledge - unlike some fundamentalists who close their minds against the evidence for evolution, for example." Take them to Colossians 2:8, Proverbs 30:6, and 1 Corinthians 1:18-23.

Note: remember, let the Word do the work. Don't force people to agree who don't want to. They must respond to the "pricking" of the Word of God, not to you!

3. The Catholics will claim continuous progress, using words such as "journey theology." They may speak of Thomas Merton's book, "*Seven Story Mountain*," or the stages in the castle of Theresa of Avila. They will tell you that they grow in holiness in the many things that they do. Mother Teresa of Calcutta just radiates grace, they say, as did Francis of Assisi and Pope John XXIII. They will be horrified to think that anyone could dare think that these are not dear saints of God. A typical statement is, "We cooperate with grace; we do not claim a one-moment salvation, as do the fundamentalists."

The underlying thought behind all the above is that people add to the good merits of Christ by our own good works, thus advancing little by little. Your response can be from Romans 11:6, Galatians 2:21, and Philippians 3:3!

4. Show the graciousness of grace (Romans 3:24), and that salvation is only by Christ alone (Hebrews 1:3; 10:10, 18).

II. Conclusion

A. Always place emphasis on the Bible as the basis of truth and that salvation is only by the gift of God's grace. If we are trying to merit (earn) salvation, then we are only invalidating God's way!

B. Always use only the exact words of Scripture.

C. Always pray - pray without ceasing - for wisdom.[12]

---

12 www.biblebc.com

Deborah Nembhard-Colquhoun

Quick Tips: Witnessing to a Jehovah's Witness

By Jason Carlson and Ron Carlson

"When teaching on the cults, rarely do we encounter someone who hasn't had a Jehovah's Witness come knocking on their front door. The Jehovah's Witnesses are notorious for their aggressive door-to-door evangelistic strategy. And while many people might view the Jehovah's Witnesses at their door as an annoyance, they are literally a mission field at our doorstep. Therefore, we try to encourage Christians to view their visits as an opportunity, an opportunity to open their eyes to the truth and to share the gospel of Jesus Christ with them.

The next time the Jehovah's Witnesses comes to your front door, instead of simply turning them away, why not spend five minutes and sow some simple seeds of truth into their lives? You may not convert them to true Christianity right there at your doorstep, but you can give them some important truths to consider, truths which may eventually bear genuine fruit of repentance and conversion in their lives.

The basic error of the Jehovah's Witnesses is what we call a "theology of denial". Jehovah's Witnesses basically deny all of the central doctrines of the Christian faith; most significantly, they deny the Deity of Jesus Christ. Jehovah's Witnesses wrongly believe that Jehovah alone is God almighty, Jesus is only a god-created being (actually the archangel Michael), and the Holy Spirit is simply an active force. This is a far cry from the true biblical doctrines of the Trinity and the Deity of Jesus Christ.

Now, if you only have five minutes to spend with a Jehovah's Witness, try walking them through the following passages of scripture, passages that bear witness to the reality of the Deity of Jesus Christ (and the beauty of sharing these passages is that you can even use the Jehovah's Witness' false version of the Bible, the *New World Translation*):

1) Begin by reading with the Jehovah's Witness from Revelation 1:8.

"I am the Alpha and the Omega," says the Lord God, "Who is, and who was, and who is to come, the Almighty."

After reading this verse together, ask them the following question, "Who is the Alpha and the Omega?" They will respond by saying something like,

"Well, it says right there, the Alpha and the Omega is the Lord God (or Jehovah God in their translation)."

2) Next, ask them if they will read another passage of scripture with you, and read from Revelation 22:13.

"I am the Alpha and the Omega, the First and the Last, the Beginning and the End"

After reading this verse with them, ask them, "Now, who exactly is the Alpha and the Omega, the First and the Last?" And they will probably respond by saying something like, "We just saw who the Alpha and the Omega, the First and the Last is, he is the Lord God (or Jehovah God in their translation).

3) Lastly, ask them if they'll look at one more passage with you, and read with them from Revelation 1:17-18.

When I saw him, I fell at his feet as though dead. Then he placed his right hand on me and said: "Do not be afraid. I am the First and the Last (stop here and ask again, 'who is the First and the Last?'). I am the Living One; I was dead, and behold I am alive for ever and ever!"

After reading this last passage of Scripture with them, ask the Jehovah's Witness, "So, when exactly did the Lord God (or Jehovah God in their translation) die?" And most Jehovah's Witnesses will just look at that passage in bewilderment, for you have just shown them conclusively, even from their own translation, that Jesus is the Lord God (or Jehovah God). If you want to demonstrate this reality even further, read with them from Revelation 22:13 & 16, where the Alpha and the Omega says, "I, Jesus, have sent my angel to give you this testimony for the churches."

This series of passages can be a powerful tool when witnessing to a Jehovah's Witness. These passages demonstrate that Jesus Christ is the Lord God, or Jehovah God. Jesus Christ is not simply a god, a created being; he is the eternal Lord God.

The next time the Jehovah's Witnesses come to your front door, instead of simply turning them away, why not try sharing these 3 passages with them? God could use you to powerfully impact the life of a Jehovah's Witness... and it only takes five minutes!"[13]

---

13 christianministriesintl.org/articles/15.html

Witnessing to Mormons-Key Elements

The following outline is in response to the many requests we have received for a brief summary of "how to witness to Mormons." Unfortunately, there is no set formula. Each witnessing opportunity is unique and different. You must depend on the Holy Spirit to guide and direct you. But there are some basic principles you can apply, things you should or should not do, and knowledge you should have. It will not be easy, and indeed, may be very frustrating, but you should do it anyway, because the Lord has commanded it.

Our ultimate goal is to lead Mormons to a personal relationship with the one true God of the Bible. Keep in mind; they think they are worshiping Him already. It's up to you to show that they have a different God, a different Jesus (2 Cor. 11:3-4), another gospel (Gal 1:8-9), and that they are breaking the first commandment. My first approach is usually to use the Bible, see the article on the web page, "Key Verses on What the Bible Says about the Father and Son" under the main heading, "Miscellaneous Topics". If I see that this has led to Scripture ping-pong then I will abandon it for the short term. My next strategy usually is to undermine the Mormon's testimony and confidence in the Mormon organization, its teachings, official history, unique scriptures (Book of Mormon, Doctrine and Covenants, Pearl of Great Price), and biblical misinterpretations. Your skill in selecting and presenting the information is important. They must become teachable before you will make any progress. Keep in mind, you cannot make anything happen. You may only facilitate it by the information you share. The recent convert or the ignorant long time member sometimes becomes teachable when they learn about the very unique LDS teachings. Use the big question when appropriate: "If you are wrong, wouldn't you like to know it?" If the answer is a clear "no," even after you test for understanding, stop witnessing.

Do not let all the information below "throw" you and keep you from witnessing. If, as a minimum you understand the first two major categories just below, then start witnessing and learn as you go.

Know What The Bible Says About Witnessing.
See Ezekiel 3:18-19; Matthew 28:19-20; 1 Peter 3:15; 2 Timothy 4:2-4; Hebrews 5:14; Jude 1:3; Acts 17: 1-2, 17, 18:4, 19:8-9.

Know What The Bible Says About a Different Jesus and Gospel.
See Galatians 1:8-9; 2 Corinthians 11:3-4.

Know What You Need.
a. Have a desire born of God, see Zechariah 4:6.
b. Know your own beliefs, have a solid Christian foundation based on the Bible. Do **NOT** witness if you are a baby Christian or are a spiritual baby.
c. Do **NOT** witness alone unless you have a great deal of experience. Even then, under some circumstances it never should be done. You should also consider using the occasion to train another. If possible have others praying for you.
d. Know enough about the false teachings of Mormonism to get started.

In Your Use Of The Bible:
a. Do not throw out the many clear verses on a subject for the few that seem to say just the opposite but really are difficult to understand.
b. Try to understand difficult verses in context, for example: 1 Cor. 15:29; Amos 3:7; Ezek 37:16-17.
c. The Bible repeats the important teachings for us many times. Be very cautious of isolated verses, such as 1 Corinthians 15:29.
d. ALWAYS look up Biblical verses you are given by a Mormon, even if you think you remember what they say.

How To And How Not To Witness:
1. Know the role of "feelings" (testimony) and how "feelings" for some can be a substitute for facts, knowledge and wisdom.
2. Know the subject! There is no substitute for factual, detailed knowledge. It will keep you from looking foolish and losing credibility. Try to have information organized for easy quick access. Being able to show full page copies from Mormon references is a powerful tool. Do not use rumour or folk tales. The articles off the main web page will give you a good base.
3. Never be rude or ridicule their beliefs. ALWAYS keep in mind the five P's: Prayer, Politeness, Patience, Perseverance and Power.
4. Be ready to "turn the other cheek," when you are abused verbally.

5. Pray before and after a discussion. You lead the prayer, and use it to teach Christian principles.//
6. Do give your conversion story. Tell what Jesus Christ has done for you.
7. Primarily use the King James Version of the Bible.
8. Know the meaning of Mormon terms. They sound Christian, but have different meanings. See the article off the main web page, "Mormon Terminology" under the main heading, "Background on Mormonism."
9. Know and understand that not all new and old Mormon references and authors are of equal authority and some should not be used. High status is given to statements by Mormon prophets and apostles speaking at official Mormon Church functions (especially Conferences) and/or published in Church manuals. The highest authority is the Mormon scriptures, but these are not always the clearest.
10. Don't assume that Mormons know Mormon doctrine. Expect a broad spectrum of beliefs. Many have very little knowledge and understanding. Others will know it all. Still others may know it all, but try to hide it. This is another reason why #2 above is important. It is best to say: "The Mormon Church teaches........." Do **NOT** say: "Mormons believe........."
11. Take the leadership role in discussions, and don't let them change the subject. If they try, bring it back, "We were talking about..." or "You didn't answer my question about..." Be bold but polite.
12. Don't argue or get angry. Walk away from an irrational or heated discussion.
13. Use a questioning technique. Generally, only ask questions that you know the answer to! Ask questions that will not be easy to answer and require thought: those that may challenge basic beliefs.
14. Be prepared for the case where you are divulging information never before heard or understood by the Mormon. This is where copies of the key pages from Mormon references are helpful.
15. The person you are witnessing to should provide documentation and references for their position.
16. Do not accept general statements like: "The Bible is all wrong"; "You people only deal in half truths and misrepresentations" etc. Insist on specifics and references for their objections.

17. Use a low key, soft, friendly approach. You don't want to intimidate your contacts. Don't cover too many subjects at one time if you will have more witnessing opportunities. It is better to cover a few subjects thoroughly. But, if you will only have one meeting, be bolder and cover more subjects.
18. The most important subjects to cover are the attributes of God and the plan of salvation. Do not waste time with trivia, like men on the moon.
19. Know that certain things are stumbling blocks to Mormons; i.e. tea, coffee, alcohol, tobacco, and discussion of temple activities.
20. One possible technique with Mormon missionaries is to invite them into your home for a meal. Ask them to come an hour or two early, and use this time for discussion. With the meal as an enticement they are less likely to suddenly have another appointment. Be sure they know the time you plan to eat.
21. **NEVER** pray about the Book of Mormon. We should follow 1 Thess. 5:21 and "Prove all things, hold fast that which is good;" it doesn't say anything about prayer. Do what the Bereans did in Acts 17:10-11.
22. When witnessing, do it with another person, but, one leads, the other's job is to **ONLY** help and not interrupt or change the subject.
23. Know the historical evolution of the key teachings of Mormonism. See the main heading, "Changes In Mormon Teachings" off of the main web page.
24. Test the prophets of Mormonism, as in Deut 13:1-5. Off the web page, under the main heading, "Miscellaneous Topics" see the article "False Prophecies of Joseph Smith."
25. Become familiar with the LDS Scriptures and know what changes have been made to them. See the main heading, "Changes In Mormon Teachings" off the main page for several article.
26. Know Mormon history. See the article, "Chronological History of Mormonism" under the main heading, "Background on Mormonism" off the main web page.

What Can You Do If You Are Not Well Trained Or Have Problems With Face To Face Discussions?

Set up your goals and read everything that moves you toward your goal. Watch and listen to experienced people witness to Mormons. Leave tracts in library books about Mormons. Tell your friends, relatives and co-workers what you know. Respond to articles on Mormonism with an appropriate "letter to the editor." Make sure you are loving, tactful and accurate in comparing doctrine and do not attack the Mormon people. Send copies of key pages from the references along with your letter.[14]

Judaism

To deal effectively with Jews, the worker must have a good working knowledge of the Old and New Testament and of the place of the Jews in God's plan.

Points for witnessing to Jews:

1. Show how CHRIST fulfilled the Old Testament prophesies concerning the Messiah. A Jew (Genesis 28:13, 14). Of the tribe of Judah (Micah 5:2). Of the family of David (Isaiah 11:1-10, Jeremiah 23:5, 6). Born of a virgin (Isaiah 7:14). In Bethlehem (Micah 5:2). Rejected and crucified (Psalm 22). Before the destruction of the temple (Daniel 9:26). His coming to be in humility (Isaiah 56). And in glory (Zachariah 2:5).

2. Show that the Old Testament sacrifices were done away in CHRIST and that salvation is found only in His shed blood (Hebrews 8:10cf Leviticus 17:11 with John 1:29). Show also that Moses spoke also of CHRIST (John 5:45-47).

3. Warn of the punishment meted out to those who reject CHRIST (Hebrews 10:20-29). If the Jew objects that "GOD did not marry a woman to give birth to CHRIST," answer that God is a miracle working God. (cf. Genesis 18:14 with Luke 1:37. Also Luke 1:26-35; Matthew 1:18-25). If he contends that the worship of Jesus is worshiping a man, use Genesis 18:1-2 (where one of the men was Jehovah), and Joshua 5:13-15. The objection that the doctrine of the Trinity teaches tree gods instead of one, may be answered by Genesis 1:1 where "GOD" Elohim is plural. See also Genesis 1:26 ("us", "our"). If he objects that Isaiah 53 refers not to CHRIST but suffering Israel, show that this is impossible, since the One who suffers is suffering, not for His own sins, but for those of another (Isaiah 53:4, 8, 8), and that others is suffering Israel!

---

14 http://www.frontiernet.net/-bcmmin

One who would work among Jews should be especially familiar with the Epistle to the Hebrews.[15]

Universalists

They are those who believe that all men will be saved in the final restoration of all things. The arguments to use with deniers of hell have already been given. Their main scriptures are 1 Timothy 2:3, 4 and 1 Corinthians 15:22.

The former expresses the desire of GOD's heart, but not His decree. Man's will is the determining factors. The latter verse read in its context, deal not with the reception of eternal life, but with physical resurrection.

The part played by man's will is seen in Luke 13:3, John 3:36, John 5:40. Such scriptures are 11 Thessalonians 1:7-9, Matthew 25:41-46, Revelation 20:15; 21:8 clearly show that all men will not be finally saved.[16]

Witnessing to Muslims

It has been said over the century that it is extremely difficult to win Muslims over to Christianity. Despite such an argument, I believe Christ is able to win them to Himself. I believe that one of the reasons why we find it so difficult is that we are using the wrong method. We must understand that only God, through His Holy Spirit, can draw anyone to Him. Too often we believe that pushing the Gospel down someone's throat is effective. It is certainly not effective for Muslims because they are doubtful and confused about our doctrine. It is very important for us to understand the Muslim history, culture, and beliefs in order to effectively evangelize to them.

I believe that the best method to win Muslims over to Christianity is to live the Gospel, so they can see it. When we live the Gospel, every sign and wonder will follow us. They do not want to read or hear about Jesus any more than they already have in their own doctrine. However, they will accept seeing and experiencing Him. Let's not forget that Jesus said that if He be lifted up then He will draw all men unto Himself. Yes! You may know that the Word is living and active according to Hebrews 4:12 and you are absolutely correct. However, the Word must be used appropriately and their hearts must be ready to receive it. The Word is so powerful that people

---

15 By J.O Sanders, www.baptistbiblebelievers.com
16 By J.O Sanders www.baptistbiblebelievers.com

can observe and experience it in their lives. We need to recognize that it is not what we say but it is the Holy Spirit that is going to activate the Word (the Gospel), and bring it to life. Another method that will work wonders in winning Muslims over to Christianity is process evangelism (building a relationship and extending love). Jesus practiced this style during His time here on earth. This process lays one brick at a time on the foundation.

Everyone is looking for a solution for life's problems. Jesus is still in the miracle working business. Through process evangelism they can be delivered from their real problems, through the power of God. Miracles will certainly get a Muslims' attention. This will reveal who Jesus is. Never forget that when signs and wonders follow, you give God all the glory. Mohammed cannot work miracles, but Jesus can. Do you see the picture? Jesus is mighty to save, but sometimes he will perform miracles before salvation. Remember that signs and wonders were not for the Christians, but for the unsaved. When they experience the mighty hand of God in their lives they have no other choice but to accept the source behind it.

Witnessing to Muslims should include the same principles as witnessing to any unsaved person. In addition to the above methods is prayer and allowing the Holy Spirit to guide. A detailed list can be found in the section "Do and Don'ts". Witnessing to cults is also in this evangelism manual. Witnessing to Muslims should not require any special technique as we are only the worker and God is the Saviour. Psalm 127:1 says "Except the LORD build the house, they labour in vain that build it..." However, God wants us to gain wisdom so we can be well equipped. It is very beneficial to understand their history, culture, beliefs etc. "How can one enter into a strong man's house, and spoil his goods, except he first bind the strong man?" (Matthew 12:29).

Why is it difficult to win Muslims over?

There are many reasons but here are a few:

- Muslims are very well cared for within their religion. Within their religion there is a community that they belong to. In this community they lack nothing. If they lose their jobs, they do not need to worry because everything will be taken care of for them.
- Muslims spend much of their time studying the Quran and they are knowledgeable of Islamic doctrine, which includes terrible punishment if they believe any other belief system.

- Muslims believe Christianity is wrong.

Let's first briefly look at their history in order to identify more methods in winning Muslims over to Christianity:

- Muslims believe that their religion is derived from their founder Mohammed, who they believed had a special vision from some sort of angelic being whom they called Gabriel.
- They claimed that this angel told Mohammed that there is only one God who is eternal, sovereign, the creator, and his name is Allah. And they are to worship him alone.
- They believe that Allah created the angels. These angels were invisible and carried out Allah's orders.
- They believe in all the prophets of the Bible and Muhammad was the last prophet of God.
- They believe that God revealed himself to man in the Torah, the Psalms, the Gospel (Injil), and the Quran.
- They believe in the Quran, which they claimed is the revelation word of Allah. They claim that it is the last book of God's revelation. In it they find God's final testament for mankind. Every other holy book is somewhat true to them, except over time that God manipulated them with false teachings and that only the Quran is free from any error.
- They believe in the last days of Judgment, the resurrection of everyone for judgment into hell or paradise.
- They believe in the predestination of Allah.

Muslim and Christianity share some similar terminology and some similar theology. Almost all of what they believe is similar to Christianity except they do not believe in a Saviour. They believe that their good works are enough to cover their sins and also that they can pray to Allah and ask him for forgiveness. Muslims practice works for their salvation while the Christians depend upon God's grace by faith for their salvation.

How do Muslims believe that they are saved?

1. They make confession of their faith to Allah. There is no other God but Allah and Mohammed is his prophet.

2. They must pray to Allah five times a day.
3. They must do good deeds to others by giving money to the poor.
4. They fast during their religion practices, such as Ramadan.
5. Every Muslim must make a pilgrimage to Mecca at least once in their life time.

Muslims view of Jesus

Muslims believe that Jesus was a prophet of God but the Quran restores the teachings of Jesus. They also believe in the virgin birth, His miracles, and that He is still alive today. They believe in most of the facts about Jesus in part, yet completely deny the most important truth, that Jesus is the Saviour of mankind. Muslims do not believe that Jesus died on the cross to save mankind of their sins. They believe that before He was killed, God took him up into heaven where he is today waiting to come back for the final Judgment. At that time He will confirm to the world that the Muslim religion is the true religion.

Muslims have many misconceptions about Christian beliefs. For example, they deny the authenticity of the Scriptures, the consistency of God's revelation, and the Trinity. They do not believe that Jesus died on the cross. Below are scriptures that will help you to witness to Muslims.

1. "For God so loved the world, that he gave his only begotten Son, that whosoever believeth in him should not perish, but have everlasting life" (John 3:16).
2. "Jesus saith unto him, I am the way, the truth, and the life: no man cometh unto the Father, but by me" (John 14:6).
3. "For unto us a child is born, unto us a son is given: and the government shall be upon his shoulder: and his name shall be called Wonderful, Counselor, The mighty God, The everlasting Father, and The Prince of Peace" (Isaiah 9:6).
4. For had ye believed Moses, ye would have believed me; for he wrote of me. But if ye believe not his writings, how shall ye believe my words?" (John 5:46-47).
5. "And he shall send Jesus Christ, which before was preached unto you: Whom the heaven must receive until the times of restitution of all things, which God hath spoken by the mouth of all his holy prophets

since the world began. For Moses truly said unto the fathers, A prophet shall the Lord your God raise up unto you of your brethren, like unto me; him shall ye hear in all things whatsoever he shall say unto you" (Acts 3:20-22).

6. "Behold, a virgin shall be with child, and shall bring forth a son, and they shall call his name Emmanuel, which being interpreted is, God with us" (Matthew 1:23).

7. "And, behold, they brought to him a man sick of the palsy, lying on a bed: and Jesus seeing their faith said unto the sick of the palsy; Son, be of good cheer; thy sins be forgiven thee. And, behold, certain of the scribes said within themselves, this man blasphemeth. And Jesus knowing their thoughts said, "Wherefore think ye evil in your hearts? For whether is easier, to say, thy sins be forgiven thee; or to say, arise, and walk? But that ye may know that the Son of man hath power on earth to forgive sins? Then saith he to the sick of the palsy, arise, take up thy bed, and go unto thine house." (Matthew 9:2-6).

8. "Nevertheless I tell you the truth; it is expedient for you that I go away: for if I go not away, the Comforter will not come unto you; but if I depart, I will send him unto you. And when he is come, he will reprove the world of sin, and of righteousness, and of judgment" (John 16:7-8).

9. "And without controversy great is the mystery of godliness: God was manifest in the flesh, justified in the Spirit, seen of angels, preached unto the Gentiles, believed on in the world, received up into glory" (1Timothy 3:16).

10. "For the prophecy came not in old time by the will of man: but holy men of God spake as they were moved by the Holy Ghost" (2Peter 1:21).

The Cult Church

The very church that we attend could be a cult church. How do we identify one? In order to witness effectively, to impart, to give wisdom and understanding to the followers we must first know how cults work; their techniques; why people join them, and how to come out of a cult.

Cults are: those who deviate from Biblical teaching in any form. Some cults are Mormons, Jehovah Witnesses, Muslims, and even within the body of the Christian churches.

How do we identify a cultic church?

- Anyone that puts themselves on equal level with Christ.
- Leaders who extol their superiority over others.
- Those that present themselves as being God's chosen one and that through them great blessings will flow, especially for their followers.
- The leaders claim that there is no one in this world who is more powerful than themselves.
- Leaders who instill fear into their followers in order to control.
- Cult leaders can be very charming. They will praise you because they are experts at pretending to be loving and are very convincing.
- They will prey on your weak areas in order to lure you.
- They are the only one with new insight to God's plan and purpose.
- The leaders will claim that God has revealed things to them that He has never revealed to anyone else.
- They are more spiritual than anyone else.
- Leaders that do not allow their followers to grow spiritually.
- Leaders who refuse to provide certain Biblical teaching to their followers so they can be enlighten with "the truth."
- They do not allow their followers to participate in other Christian involvement or even visit other Bible believing church events.
- Leaders who restrain their followers from making independent, spiritual and rational decisions.
- Induce guilt with confusion and self criticism toward their followers.
- If you are not in agreement with the leader, there must be something wrong with you. You must agree with the leader even if you are agreeing with sin.
- Regardless of all the other churches, their church is the one true church.
- They will announce that if you leave their church something bad will happen to you.

- Leaders often tell their followers that they are not growing; while on the other hand they will tell them that they are very powerful, have special gifts and are even more spiritually mature than anyone else.
- Today they will often openly embarrass you and tomorrow praise you in secret.
- The leaders make every decision for you therefore the growth of the followers are stifled.

Why is it hard to get out?
- When you are in a cult you are in an extended family.
- You find instant love and friendship that will disappear upon leaving them.
- The leaders will keep the followers so busy with events and activities within their organization that they will become too busy even to think for themselves.
- Their followers often are like robots because they are often brainwashed.
- The leaders usually work on their followers emotional, psychological, and social needs.
- Their followers are often living in fear and intimidation.
- Unless the Holy Spirit opens the spiritual eyes of those who are under the cultic spell they will not even believe that they are in a cultic church.
- Manipulated and brainwashed.
- Fear of rejection, fear of the unknown, obligation, pride, and confusion.

How to leave a cult?
- Run for your life.
- It is necessary to leave once you are convinced that you are in a cult and are violating God's will. However, that is easier said than done. It can be very hard to come out but where there is a will there is a way.
- In order to come out, you must first choose who you will serve, man or God?

- Being part of such a group will lead to negative consequences.
- Seek support from other Christians.
- Associate yourselves with Godly people and those who will give you Godly counsel, encouragement, love, and care.
- Ask God to take you out and adhere to his leading.
- Give no indication to the cult leaders or other followers that you are aware that they are a cult and that you are planning to leave.
- Understand that Christ is the one responsible for your salvation and that no man can give you the salvation that Christ gives.

Why people join cults?

- Lack of knowledge of the Word or God.
- A sense of belonging.
- Human need to part of a group or community.
- The need for acceptance.
- Searching for love.
- Searching for truth.
- The enemy has deceived them, blinding their eyes to the truth.
- Searching for emotional stimulation.
- Love being entertained.
- Love self-gratification.
- Financial, emotional, and social needs.
- Seeking for safety and security.
- A sense of loyalty.
- Sometimes low self-esteem.
- Others make decision for them.
- Looking for purpose.
- Naivety.

If you are in a church and you recognize that it is a cult. I beg you to run for your life, before it is too late. Not only will this involvement compromise your salvation, it will take away your joy, peace, and blessing in Christ and it will also cause you to lose your soul into eternal damnation.

Additional information on Cults

The "Jesus" of the Cults

By Ron Carlson and Jason Carlson (Christian Ministries International)

In Matthew chapter 24, Jesus' disciples came to him and asked, "Tell us, when will this happen, and what will be the sign of your coming and of the end of the age?" In responding to this question, it's very interesting what Jesus identified as the foremost sign of his second coming and of the end of the age, "Watch out that no one deceives you. For many will come in my name, claiming, 'I am the Christ,' and will deceive many."

Today we are seeing the fulfillment of this warning sign as never before. Our world is literally flooded with false "christs" and false messiahs. It is estimated that there are over 1,000 cults in America alone with some 25-30 million followers! And each of these false cults promotes their own man-made version of "Jesus Christ" who is not the Jesus of the Bible.

So, who is the "Jesus" of the cults?

Jehovah's Witnesses say that Jesus is actually Michael, the Archangel. He was the first creation of God. He came to Earth as a man, died on a stake, and rose from the grave invisibly as a spirit. Jesus then returned invisibly to Brooklyn, N.Y. in 1914 to head-up the Watchtower Bible and Tract Society.

Mormons (The Church of Jesus Christ of Latter Day Saints) teach that Jesus is the spirit brother of Satan. He was once a human being like you and I, but through good works he evolved spiritually to become a god. However, Jesus is just one god amongst a pantheon of gods, all of who were once human and evolved to become gods themselves. Jesus was born to Mary through physical incest when his father god had sexual relations with her. And Mormons teach that the blood and cross of Christ is foolishness and cannot fully atone for our sins (ever notice how there's no cross on any Mormon church or temple?).

Christian Science and Mary Baker Eddy say that Jesus was only a man and that Christ is a Divine idea. Furthermore, Jesus never did any supernatural miracles; he simply showed people their mental illusions of sin, evil, illness and disease. Christian Science says that Jesus did not die and his resurrection was only in a spiritual sense.

Sun Myung Moon (the Korean messiah) claims that Jesus was a man who failed his divine mission and he, Rev. Moon, is the second coming of Christ to unite the world under the banner of the Unification Church.

The **Baha'i** say that Jesus is only one of nine great world manifestations; he is not a unique path to salvation and all religions are basically the same.

Unitarians believe that Jesus was a good man who was mistakenly deified by his followers.

Freemasonry teaches that Jesus was only a moral teacher. He was no better than Buddha, Confucius, Moses or Mohammed. They deny that Jesus was the light of the world and claim that Freemasonry is the true light of humanity.

Scientology and L. Ron Hubbard claim that Jesus is a false dream.

Spiritists say that Jesus is an advanced medium in the 6th sphere of the astrological projection (wherever that is?).

Unity teaches that Jesus is a man who perfected a divine idea.

Rosicrucians claim that Jesus is a manifestation of cosmic consciousness.

Maharishi and Transcendental Meditation says that Jesus was an enlightened guru who never suffered or died for anyone.

The more you study the false cults, the more you realize that the "Jesus" of the cults is not the Jesus of the Bible. All of the cults promote their own false, man-made versions of Jesus Christ; they are counterfeits and cannot save anyone.

So, who is the real Jesus?

In John 1:1 we read, "In the beginning was the Word (Jesus), and the Word was with God, and the Word was God." A few verses later in John 1:14 we learn, "The Word became flesh and made his dwelling among us. We have seen his glory, the glory of the One and Only, who came from the Father, full of grace and truth."

In Colossians 1:15 Paul tells us that Jesus "is the visible image of the invisible God…" In Colossians 2:9 Paul says, "For in Christ all the fullness of the Deity lives in bodily form…"

The real Jesus is the one true God of all creation. He is the second person of the eternal Triune Godhead. He loves us so much that He broke into human history and split history into B.C. and A.D. to personally reveal Himself to us. The Bible says that Jesus came to "seek and to save the lost" (Luke 19:10; John 3:16-17; Ephesians 2:8-9). And as Acts 4:12 declares, "Salvation is found in no one else, for there is no other name under heaven given to men by which we must be saved."[17]

Religion vs. Christianity: What's the difference?

By Jason Carlson and Dr. Ron Carlson of CMI

"Why are you Christians always sending missionaries overseas? People have their own culture, their own religion, why don't you just leave them alone?!" This is one of the most common statements we hear as we lecture on college and university campuses throughout the United States and around the world. Students and faculty often jeeringly ask us, "What is so special about Christianity, different from every religion in the world?" To be sure, this is a very significant question; and probably one of the most significant questions that any Christian could ask themselves: what is so special about Jesus Christ?

Our family has a close friend named Lou. Lou grew up in the nation of Thailand and he was a Buddhist for the first 20 years of his life until he met some Christian missionaries who introduced him to Jesus Christ. If you were to ask Lou today, "What is so special about Jesus Christ and Christianity different from every other religion in the world?" Lou would share with you the following story:

"When I was a Buddhist I felt like I was in the middle of a large lake. I was drowning and I didn't know how to swim. As I struggled to keep my head above water, I looked out towards the shore and saw Buddha walking up to the edge of the lake. I was going under for the third time, when suddenly Buddha began shouting out instructions to me, teaching me how to swim. Buddha shouted, 'Kick your legs and paddle your arms.' But then Buddha said, 'Lou, you must make it to shore by yourself.' As I desperately struggled to follow the instructions of Buddha, I looked out towards the shore again, but this time I saw Jesus Christ walking towards the edge of the lake. However, Jesus did not stop at the edge of the lake. Jesus dove into the lake and he swam out and rescued me! And once Jesus

---

17 website www.Jude3.com

had brought me safely back to shore, then he taught me how to swim, so that I could go back and rescue others!"

You see, this is the key difference between Christianity and every other religion in the world: Christianity is not a religion! What are religions? Religions are about human attempts to make our lives right with God, through our good works, sacrifices, rituals, and money. However, Christianity is not a religion. Christianity is about God entering human history to graciously save men and women through His Son Jesus Christ. It is only by placing our faith in Jesus Christ and submitting to his Lordship that we will be saved.

A relationship with God will never be found in any religion, because religions only offer swimming lessons to people drowning in the sea of sin. And it doesn't matter how sincere or devout you are in your religious faith and practice, because the sea of sin is eternally immense. The only hope for men and women drowning in the sea of sin is Jesus Christ. God entered human history in the person of Jesus Christ; he dove into the sea of sin in order to save desperate and drowning people. If you'll allow him to take you there, he'll hold you in his loving arms and bring you safely to shore. And after arriving safely to shore, then your swimming lessons begin, so that you can go back and rescue others![18]

---

18 website www.Jude3.com

19

CREATION VS. EVOLUTION

When being confronted by those who believe in evolution over creation it is very good to understand both. I have looked at both and make my argument below.

I believe in creation vs. evolution, not only because of my knowledge and faith in God but also because of the evidence in the universe and the many facts in Scripture that explain creation. The creativity and wondrous work behind this universe gives me all the reason to believe that a divine God is responsible for creation. One theory of Evolution states that this world was form by a "big bang." They also believe that all life arose from a few simple forms. When you compare the belief of creation versus evolution, believing creation doesn't require you to be a genius, it is just common sense.

Evolutionists believe that life is the product of random chance. They hold that, "million of years ago lifeless matter, acted upon by natural forces, gave origin to one or more minute living organisms which have since evolved into living and extinct plants and animals including man."[19] How sensible is this? No wonder scientists are working so hard to find alternative ways of creating human beings. God has not stopped creating life, but is constantly doing so every second. No other being or source can produce life; all they are doing is working with the life source already created by God who is the source of all life. Life, in my understanding, could only be explained by an intelligent means with God is behind it. This fact is also a universally recognized truth. Only those who are truly with no knowledge of God could think life came from random chance. It is almost impossible for one not to have any knowledge of God because the universe declares the works of a Creator (God). The Scriptures also tell us that God gave humans

---

19 Evoltion: A handbook for Students by a Medical Scientist (Toronto: International Christian Crusade, 1951), p.7.

consciousness of Himself in their hearts. Therefore, it is man's choice to believe in any other source than God in the creation of the universe. God is revealed in the Bible to be the Creator of all things (John 1:3; Hebrews 1:1-3), and He is the God of all and the Head over all things, including science (Acts 10:36; Ephesians 1:22).

The creativity we see in the universe can only be the product of a creative being. This fact is not only in scriptures but is also supported by some scientist. Studies conducted by college psychologist, Bryn Mawr, "found that 40% of American scientists believe in a personal God." In 1996, and again in 1998, Pulitzer prize winner Professor Edward Larson of the University of Georgia, and Washington Times reporter, Larry Witham, teamed up to duplicate Leuba's study in an effort to determine if scientists' religious beliefs have changed much over the last 65 years. Larson and Witham found that 40% of American scientists still believe in a personal God."[20]

In creation we see the existence of a sovereign Creator who expressed and exercised His great creative abilities. From the earth's viewpoint, creation is like a canvas. At the top we see the beautiful, humongous, breath-taking blue skies with different elements. On the surface we see intricate details of creative things made up of living organisms…the universe is a masterpiece indeed. The creativity, splendor, greatness, majesty, glory, and wondrous works behind this universe give me all the reason to believe in creation and not evolution. Psalm 19:1 says that "The heavens declare the glory of God; and the firmament sheweth his handywork." There is no limit to this creation and our finite mind can never comprehend it. Therefore, we should have no other choice but to put the infinite God behind it.

In man's ability we can see this same creativity, except it is limited. Each and every human being exhibits some sort of creativity yet none have the capacity to produce such masterpieces (the universe) like God has. When you analyze God's art, it is not simple, it is extremely complex. As a matter of a fact, the more we know about our reality, the more we understand its infinite complexity. Psalm 8:3 says, "When I consider thy heavens, the work of thy fingers, the moon and the stars, which thou hast ordained." "God has left His fingerprints on the universe. Every rock, every tree, every river, every ocean, and every star in the sky— they all bear the Divine DNA that points back to God who created all things."[21]

---

20 allaboutcreation.org/scientists-who-believe-in-god
21 Verse by Verse, With Pastor Don Mckay at 1st Baptist Church of Gold Beach

How it is possible that an impersonal random force produces a product that exhibits intelligence, design, order and purpose which the random force itself does not possess? The universe is full of evidence of intelligent design and where you have intelligent design, isn't it logical to believe that there is an intelligent designer? I believe it is and I believe that designer to be God. There is also enough scientific evidence to support a designer. Either all of the universe which includes: space, matter, energy, time, light, life, consciousness, rationality, etc. is the result of God the Creator or is random matter. If someone is inclined to believe that the entire world with all its glorious diversity of life just happened, then no amount of evidence will be enough to prove the existence of a Creator. The creative intellectual ability that I was created with points me to a Creator of the universe. A little of God's DNA is in every human being. This is why we are creative, knowledgeable; intelligent…no amount of random matter could produce such abilities.

It is really a joke to believe that the universe was created by matter. Everything that makes up the universe not only requires an intelligent creator but a supernatural intervention. With such a universe in place, how could matter be intelligent enough to cause a universe to come into existence? Also, who created that matter in the first place? There is no power in matter to cause the universe to be self-contained, self-maintained and exist as an eternal system.

Evolution assumes that the universe was the result of a "big bang." This is not in agreement with the Bible. Genesis 1 describes all the physical events of creation. Pay no attention to other causes of creation; anything outside God is invalid because there is no knowledge outside God. Psalm 111:10 declares, "The fear of the Lord is the beginning of wisdom." Proverbs 1:7 says, "The fear of the Lord is the beginning of knowledge." If one does not know God, it is hard for him to believe in creation. I believe in creation because I have the knowledge of God and this is the reason I can understand Genesis 1:1; "In the beginning God created the heavens and the earth." It makes more sense to believe that the universe was created by an intelligent being rather than out of matter. How else do we explain the universe appearing out of nothing? Can something come out of nothing? Of course not, therefore, this is where a supernatural sovereign God comes in. He is the only one who can create something out of nothing. The universe must have had to be created; it is impossible in the physical for a universe to just appear out of nowhere.

Psalms 14:1 proclaims that those who deny God are "fools." 1 Corinthians 2:14 states, "But the natural man receiveth not the things of the Spirit of God: for they are foolishness unto him: neither can he know them, because they are spiritually discerned." Yes, the Spirit of God gives us knowledge to know the truth; however, we need no special revelation to believe the truth of creation because the universe shows forth the creative works of God. The universe not only paints a picture of creation, but also preaches a sermon about the wonders of our great God. In Psalm 19:1 we read that God has revealed Himself in creation: "The heavens declare the glory of God; and the firmament showeth his handywork." We also read in Romans 1:19, 20 that "which may be known of God is manifest.... For since the creation of the world His invisible attributes are clearly seen, being understood by the things that are made, even His eternal power and Godhead."

The book of Genesis told us that God created the earth, all its creatures and the first man and woman. Evolutionists rely on genetics to understand such process. When we take the side of creation we are claiming that God is responsible for life on earth, while evolution proposes that life has evolved over billions of years. The beginning of creation lines up with the Word of God. Creation goes beyond the reach of science. There are no experiments that can test when the universe began; the Bible is a reputable and proven source of evidence of when creation began. Not according to the "big bang," but according to Scriptures, our universe is roughly 6,000 years old, dating back to the time of Adam's creation (Genesis 1:1). Through biblical facts and through faith we believe that this mysterious universe was created. God was actively involved in creation at the beginning and is still involved.

Conclusion:

Many believe in evolution, however, a biblical investigation, Gods redemptive plan, and the evidence of Gods hands in the universe eliminate that possibility. Evolution comes from man who is driven by the enemy who is trying to rob God of His glory. When we believe in creation over evolution we are acknowledging the works of God.

20

BIBLE DOCTRINES IN A NUTSHELL

We will perish for lack of knowledge (Hosea 4:6). To have total security and to be effective in sharing the Gospel, an individual must have a complete knowledge of Biblical doctrines, which include the doctrine of the entire Bible, the doctrine of God, Christ, the Holy Spirit, man, salvation, angels, Satan, demons, the church, and the last days.

One cannot truly understand Christianity until they understand the Word of God. This is because the Word of God is Christ; therefore, Christ is the foundation of Christianity. The Bible says, "In the beginning was the Word...and the Word was made flesh and dwelt among us" (John 1: 1, 14). Christ is the Good News for mankind which was created in the image of God but got disconnected because of sin. No matter how we satisfy the human flesh, there is an inner need to connect to God which is the spiritual part of man (the image of God). Jesus Christ is the solution for this inner need. This is why the Word of God says that we are complete when we receive Christ. We were dead in trespasses and sin, but become alive by the Spirit of God (through Christ). The Bible says, "God is a spirit: and they that worship him must worship him in spirit and in truth" (John: 4:24). How do we show forth the Spirit of God? I believe by demonstrating the fruit of the Spirit which are love, joy, peace... The Bible says we are not of Him if we don't have the Spirit of God (Romans: 8). We had His Spirit before our first parents allowed the enemy to suck it out of us. We were able to communicate with the Holy God before the fall of mankind. We lost all that and have a need for a Saviour. Jesus Christ comes and blows back the Spirit of God into us through His death, burial, and resurrection and through us when we demonstrate our faith in Him. Here we see that Christianity is more than just identifying ourselves as Christians without any real truth behind it, Christianity involves knowing biblically who God is, knowing and believing the purpose for which He sent His Son, taking on Christ, which includes His attributes, and having a right relationship with God.

Faith is one of the keys in understanding God. We are able to function in our daily lives because of faith. This is called daily faith. However, faith can be categorized as doctrinal faith, saving faith, and the gift of faith. When we have an understanding of Christ, we receive salvation through faith. We become justified by God, not because of any thing we do, but through our faith. In this act, all that is required is that we believe that we are declared righteous. In our flesh, we have limited faith, but when Christ (the Holy Spirit) dwells in us, our faith can be limitless if we allow Him to control our being. Sometimes I wonder how some Christians are able to do so much through Christ while having so little experience with God, and then I realize that although we all have a measure of faith, and faith is deposited in our hearts as we study the Word of God, not all have been given the gift of faith. A good thing about God is that what He does for others He can do for us. If we desire the gift of faith, we can receive it by praying and believing that God is able to do more than we can ever ask or think.

There is no doubt that the Word of God is true. How can we be sure? God has provided revelation and inspiration to interpret and understand the truth of His Word. The record of history, nature, and our consciences are means by which God reveals Himself. However, the Scripture is one of the most important means by which God reveals Himself. If it wasn't for God's revealed Word, the Bible, we would not have the doctrine which teaches us and leads us to salvation. We are able to live a righteous life while looking towards eternal life because of the revealed Word of God. You see, revelation is God communicating things to us we could not otherwise know except that He reveals it to us. God is such a detailed and loving God. He also provides illumination by His Spirit which takes us from understanding the Word to having a relationship with Him. God is an all-knowing God. He knows the sinful nature of man's heart so He protected His revealed Word to teach us without any error by divine inspiration. This truth that the Word is divinely inspired is not just proven based on the accurate facts and evidence of the Bible but it has also been proven by many Christians and non Christians of high caliber who have done much research. The Bible tells us that it was the Holy Spirit who led the men of old to write the Scriptures. Peter: 1:21 and John: 16:13-15 both say that the Spirit is the one who leads us into all truth. Much evidence can be found through Scripture. He inspired authors by revelation, by dreams, visions, symbols, His actual voice, dictation, eyewitness reports, and Jesus Christ. Despite the means that were used, the words were what He wanted them to write.

God is infinite; therefore, the finite mind can never comprehend who God is. Therefore, how can we truly explain who He is? Ps.: 145:1-3 tells us that His greatness is unsearchable; no one can comprehend Him. The Holy Spirit gives us a vivid description of God in His Word. This is because our understanding is limited. The Bible tell us that God is a Spirit (John 4:24), which makes Him supernatural, sovereign with unlimited power (Gen 18:25), unchangeable (Heb: 1:12), and He is everywhere (Ps 139). He existed before creation, He is the source of all living things, and He is eternal, without sin. Without Him everything would be dead. He has many attributes which are important for us to know so that we can line ourselves up to His laws. John 1 tells us that He is love; Isa. 6 says that He is Holy. As Christians, all our attributes of holiness, justice, goodness, truth and love come from the only source, God. If we don't know God, we are lost forever. This is why studying the Scriptures is important. Without knowing what the Word says, we will violate God's law and put ourselves in danger. A mystery to man is how God is one, yet manifests Himself as three persons at the same time. The Godhead of the Trinity lays a foundation for all the doctrines we believe. The Father, Son, and Holy Spirit are always in unity with each other as they each play a part in our lives. Behind the Creator of this world with every thing in it, we can see a supernatural creator. We can also see God through Jesus Christ and the Word of God. Jesus Christ is the centre of all Christian faith who reveals God by His Spirit. God's love for us is more than we can ever imagine. The proof of His love is how He created us in His image Gen. 1 gives us the opportunity to know about Him; despite our sins, He gives us another chance to share in His existence now and in eternity. We don't have to lack anything through Christ. God can be anything we want Him to be. He will do anything we ask as long as it is lined up to His Word. It is important that we know the Word so we can use it by faith. Not only does He place us in His plan but He revealed Himself through many names. He provides the name Jehovah for example, which means the I am who I am (Ex. 3:14).

God came in flesh so that man could relate to Him. If He came in the spirit alone we would not be able to comprehend Him. There has never been a human being who ever lived or will ever live that can compare to Jesus Christ. He is the Prophet of all prophets, the Priest of all priests (Heb 7), who is making intercession for us. He is the Kings of all kings (Rev 15:3), whose kingdom is in heaven. John 18:3-6; He is the only begotten son of God. He is the only one who was ever supernaturally inseminated in a womb, and the only one who can atone for man's sins. He is the sinless Lamb who is the only true foundation of biblical doctrine. The work Christ has done has baffled the minds of many. No one could do the miracles He did. He went through extreme agony; no one has ever gone through or will ever go through the extent of His agony, yet He did not sin. One of the mysteries about Him was that He was one hundred percent man and one hundred percent sovereign God at the same time. This is one of many mysteries that show that He is God. If we could truly comprehend it without any biblical knowledge, we would be on the same level as God. God can be anything He wants to be. God is God all by Himself. God is altogether holy and man is sinful. If God came in all His glory, we wouldn't be able to look upon Him and live. Also He came through man to deliver the fatal blow to Satan, since it was man who Satan deceived. The truth about Jesus is not a fairy tale but a reality. His deity was foretold years before His arrival in Mary's womb. He came to earth and demonstrated His deity and is still operating today in the lives of Christians (1 Cor. 6:9). Because He came in human form, we see that He loves us and will continue to dwell in our bodies through the Holy Spirit as long as we keep it clean from sin. Jesus lives forever. He is now at the right hand side of God making intercession for us and will live with us forever if we accept Him as our Saviour.

One part of the Godhead, God the Holy Spirit, might be viewed as a myth or might even be looked upon as of not much importance. However, the Spirit of God is active and well. He is the key to understanding the Word of God, thus enabling us to do His will and live a successful life. The Word of God itself was established by an intelligent being which is the Holy Spirit. Man is in absolute darkness without the Holy Spirit. It might appear as though we are functioning in our own strength, but we are only strong when we are functioning in the Holy Spirit. The Holy Spirit is the source of all power and this is because the Holy Spirit is the sovereign God. The Scripture says that no one has ever seen God. This is because He is spirit, and so we worship Him not because we are able to see Him but by faith through the conviction of the Holy Spirit who guides us into all truth. The Holy Spirit has intellect and emotion just as we do; therefore, we need to be sensitive not to grieve Him. The way we grieve Him is by allowing sin into our lives. We can depend on the Spirit completely to live a perfect, righteous life. Once we tap into the Holy Spirit, we are able to do great exploits, even beyond our human understanding. It was the Holy Spirit who performed the many works through Jesus in Bible days, and is still responsible for the many great works being done today in and through the lives of believers. As God the Father and God the Son will never die, so God the Spirit is immortal because they are one.

God came in flesh with His own soul and worked in oneness, but man is flesh and is operating with a borrowed soul. Man is not just dust. The physical body is not the total man. The Bible says that we were created in the image of God. After we were formed out of the dust, God blew breath into man, who then became a living soul with a living body (Gen. 1). This is why we are able to function like Christ with intellect, emotions, will, and moral consciousness which are all derived from God. Our physical body was created to be permanent but became temporary. This is because sin has polluted it. The body will die as a result while the soul will never die. Whether we go to heaven or hell, it will never die. The soul is what is keeping the body alive. We need to live by the Spirit so we can stay spiritually alive and if we become physically dead we will then go to heaven. If we are spiritually dead without any resurrected body, we will go to hell. When our soul leaves our body, our body is dead. James 2:26 says, "The body without the spirit is dead." Thanks be to God that as children of God we are joint heirs with Christ. This means that we are not only entitled to all His blessings through His redeeming work for us, but we will also receive a new body for our soul that is in the image of God. This will allow us to live forever with Him. We were given freedom by God but with restrictions. This is because limited wisdom, power, and self-restraint were given to us. We went out of the limits and as a result brought death upon ourselves. Despite our sinful nature, our personalities are derived from God. Therefore, we are able to make the conscious decision to not detour any more from God's law and stop yielding to the enemy's trickeries. If, by salvation, we take back the image of God, then we are able like Jesus (who is the image of God) to resist the enemy and he will flee from us.

Upon receiving salvation, the evidence of man's role in salvation and God's perspective must be visible. The old nature of sin should be changed. At this point, we are no more slaves to sin, but have been transformed into a new creature (2 Cor: 5:17). During this process of conversion and regeneration, we become conscious of our sinful nature, realizing that we need a Saviour, and ask, by faith believing, that God through His Spirit would change us. When this is exercised, our bodies become empowered by the Holy Spirit that is living within us. We are no longer dead but immediately become alive, connecting us back to God who declares us righteous. We are also qualified to perform His works, and partake of His abundant blessing, in this life and the eternal life to come.

One of our earthly blessings is that God has assigned innumerable angels to assist us in the physical and spiritual realm. The Word of God says the angel of the Lord encamps around those that fear Him and delivers them (Ps 34:7). Who are these angels? When we study the doctrine of angels we see that they are similar to God and man. They are spiritual beings, made a little higher than man and very much lower than God. Angels are spiritual forces but are not all powerful, all present, or all knowing as God is (Ps 103:20). They were created by God (Ps 148:2) to serve Him (Isa. 6:3). They were also given personalities (intellect, emotion, and will) which make them able to operate like us, except in a higher capacity. We are limited as human beings, therefore, what we cannot do; they are available to assist us. We must feel reassured that, although we might not be able to fight the spiritual forces that are against us, we are not alone because we have angels to help and protect us.

We must not think of ourselves higher than we ought to think but recognize that God alone is God, who chooses to give us personality, intellect, emotions, and wills. Through the free will that God has given angels and man, we see how easily we can deceive ourselves and neglect the Creator. As man chose to disobey God and fell (pride), so we also see disobedience among the angels. One of the greatest angels, Lucifer, was given superior intellect, but we see how he allowed his emotions (pride) to rob him of his position, and as a result, awaits eternal punishment. He is on a mission to destroy the thing that God loves and created in His image - us. We must recognize that we have an adversary (the devil) who is looking to kill, steal, and destroy. We were created perfectly without any sin but got contaminated with sin through our own free will. If we allow our will to lead us to yield to Satan's deception, we will also be lost forever with Satan and his angels who rebelled against God. Satan has no future, but thanks be to God that despite our sins, we were given another chance to have a future with God and his good angels. We can resist the enemy and he will flee. God will never leave us alone. Apart from the countless good angels He has assigned to us, is the Holy Spirit living within us to help us combat the enemy.

Satan is a created being. He is also a counterfeiter who tries to counterfeit everything that comes from God. If we are not wise, we will be tricked by his deception. What he displays before us is not always bad; when we yield to it, it is bad. He has nothing good to offer, he is the god of destruction. It is not only important to understand Satan, but also to recognize that he has demons working for him. These angels became very sinful as a result of their yielding to Satan's trickery. They too were kicked out of heaven. As children of God fulfilling his good deeds, so Satan has his angels doing wicked deeds. Some of these deeds include physical disease, mental suffering, tempting people to sin, possessing people, and conducting false teaching. These are not always caused by the enemy, however. We need to discern the difference so we can deal with them accordingly. Demons are all around us in the spiritual realm manifesting in the physical realm. Like humans, bad angels (who are demons) also have personalities (intellect, emotions, will). We are no match for them because they have tremendous power. We do need to be aware of their personalities and strength but do not need to be afraid of them, knowing that the Word of God says if God is for us who can be against us, and if we walk in God's light, we are more than conquerors through Christ who gives us strength. God is fighting all our battles for us. He has also opened up our spiritual eyes to see our enemy, and has provided weapons and help for us to fight and win. We are armed and dangerous not by ourselves, but with the help of the Holy Spirit within us. No weapon can touch God's power. We should at no time involve ourselves in any works of the devil, in such we are playing on deadly ground. Some of his associations are: divination, necromancy, magic, sorcery, witchcraft, and astrology. God has forbidden us to associate ourselves with any of these. We are not to be friends with the enemy. Our job is to attack the works of the enemy. God has given us the anointing to destroy his works (Luke 4:18).

One can chase a thousand but two will put ten thousand to flight. We are not alone but we are a body of believers world-wide joined together in love by the Spirit of God. God has a church that He has established on this earth to represent His very life. As we read the Scripture, we see that we are that church, and the gates of hell shall not prevail against us. The church might be few in number but nothing can tear it apart, its foundation is eternal. It is through this foundation (Christ) that we are sealed for eternity. The church will be caught up in the air to meet Him; therefore, we need to check ourselves with His Word to see if we are a part of His body. The Bible says we are none of His if we do not have the Spirit of God (Rom. 8:9). Time is running out and God said He is coming back for a church without spot or wrinkle. Sinful bodies have no place with God, for He is a holy God. The redeemed, blood-washed people (Christians) are the church, and when we unite together, we are able to do great exploits, not by ourselves, but through Christ who lives in us. Our purpose is to fulfill the will of God. He has provided and equipped us with all the tools we need to function. As He has put the foundation in place (Himself), so then we are part of the whole structure. Divided we fall, but together we stand. Christ has joined us together with Him. When we allow Him to control us, we will be connected to His body until He comes to take us home with Him. What He taught His disciples in the Bible was not only for those days, but also for us now, so that we can continue to carry on His work. The blueprint for how the church is to continue building and functioning can be found in the Scriptures. Souls are depending on us to lead them into the body of Christ. If we neglect to study and follow the Word of God, we are in danger with God. We as Christians might not be called to be a Pastor or a Deacon, but we have all been given gifts and their purpose is to be used in whatever capacity we can. The church is the light of the world and if we fail to shine the light in the dark world, we are not doing the will of God. Not only does the body of Christ lead sinners to salvation, but it also helps us grow and gives us blessing and victory and protection over sin.

The Bible has been proven to be God's Word from Genesis to Revelation. Although many prophecies of the future in the book of Revelation are yet to come to pass, we have seen much of God's Word fulfilled over the last century. There are many churches today, yet not all belong to Christ. We should not be amazed because this is among the many prophecies that have been foretold. The Scriptures tell us about many who will arise that don't belong to Him. There is an obvious ecumenical movement across the nation which is not of the true church. If the unity is not based upon the Word of God, it is not the true church. We must be discerning.

Let us also remember the prophecies that not only tell us about the good but also the bad. It is very good and exciting to look forward to the awesome prophecies to come, especially the one where we will be with the

Lord forever in glory having perfect joy, peace, comfort, full knowledge, no pain, no sickness, and no death. However, what about the prophecies that declare that those who doesn't belong to the Church will be lost in hell forever? It is the church's responsibility to prevent this from happening, by introducing salvation to all. The Word of God says that no one knows the time when He will return; however, He gave us clues which are the signs of the time. Look around us, the signs of the time are everywhere. He may come like a thief in the night. When we think there is peace and safety, there will come sudden destruction. If we miss His return, there will be a period of great tribulation when those who are not raptured with the church will suffer extreme agony. The possibility at this time to turn to Christ is very slim. Therefore, we should not allow such great anguish to reach us while there is still time. Let us yield to the Word and fulfill our call.

Conclusion

It is of vital importance that we understand doctrines of the Bible because they give us spiritual stability and maturity. Understanding doctrine is the key to salvation, it brings us into knowledge with God, it is the foundation for a godly life, the tool to witness, and it equips us for service. The doctrine of the Bible also opens our eyes to unsound doctrines so we can counteract it, not only in the world but also in the church.

21

CHOOSING AN INDIVIDUAL FOR MINISTRY

The most important thing we need to do when choosing anyone for ministry is to consult with God first. This means asking for God's instruction through prayer, having an inclined ear to listen to His voice and follow His instruction. In Judges 7:1-7 we read that the victory of Gideon's army was a result of this. Gideon consulted God and followed His instructions. In choosing, Gideon screened the people by putting then through a couple of tests; the fear test and the water test.

Even though we are all called to evangelize, God wants us to consult Him first before selecting an evangelism team or those who will be in a position of ministry. Isaiah 30:1 reads, "Woe to the rebellious children, saith the LORD, that take counsel, but not of me; and that cover with a covering, but not of my spirit"...Throughout the Scriptures and even in our society, we find many great teams that have failed because they refused to consult God. Once God is first in any planning and all His instructions are followed out correctly, there is a certainty for success. In Judges 7:1-7 we read how Gideon recruited and organized his army by reducing the total number of candidates (22,000) to one percent (300) as God had instructed him. See how important it is to hear from God! With human sight it looked smart to have an enormous number of candidates, as a matter of fact, with human eyes, the more the better. Our ego is just tickled by a crowd! Not so in God's eyes. God knows everything. Isaiah 55: 8-9 says, "For my thoughts are not your thoughts, neither are your ways my ways, saith the LORD". Vs. 9, "For as the heavens are higher than the earth, so are my ways higher than your ways, and my thoughts than your thoughts".

As leaders, making certain decisions might seem like the right choice. For example, choosing a group of Evangelists who are well established, recruiting many people for a particular ministry, etc. This picture might look great but what is God saying in the matter? If we consult God first, He will see the hidden things we are not able to see and reveal them to us. Although these men might seem best suited for the task, God, on the other hand, may see trouble. His choosing could be a few simple Christians who have the heart of God and will be united together. Also, when we don't rely on numbers (man's strength) we will see the hands of God. God want us to see His hands at work in His ministry and not man's.

This act of reducing Gideon's army to one percent as mentioned earlier was to demonstrate to Israel that their strength was not to come from the army, but from the all-powerful God. Isn't it amazing how God "chose the foolish things of the world to shame the wise; God chose the weak things of the world to shame the strong?" (1 Corinthians 1:27). To determine the ones who weren't qualified and the ones who were, God told Gideon to perform a couple of tests. The first was a test of courage. To be selected for evangelism, one needs courage because the sight of what you will be treading upon in the world can be very frightening. Proving those means putting them to the test. We sometimes have to put those that are working with us to a test, according to God's instruction, and allow God to remove those whom He chooses. This test might let them experience what ministry is all about. As a result of the test, we need to also embrace God's decision which might leave us with 3 people out of 30 within our ministry.

Gideon put the men to the test by allowing all the men to view the large army that they would be battling against. When they saw how many they were (like locusts) and that their camels could no more be counted than the sand on the seashore, they trembled with fear. More than half backed off. First, they had seen the impossible situation of winning. In their minds, they were losers already because of their obvious inferior number against them. They did not know that if God is for them, who could be against them? This, I believe, was a demonstration of their lack of faith in God. It is important to have faith in God when fighting against any army. They were only relying on their own strength, not on God's ability to bring them the victory. I would bet that God had placed a mighty invisible army among them, which they could not see. Without God's instruction, Gideon would not have known that they were fearful. God knew that with this kind of attitude they could not be included in the army, lest the army would be a defeated one. God is able to win any war without anyone; however, He is looking for ready vessels that have faith in Him. It is His plan for humans to play a part in Him being glorified. There are always some negative people around us in ministry who cannot see God's hands at work. They even laugh at and criticize others' vision. They have failed the test because that negative faith will cause blockage and defeat.

The second test was a test of readiness for battle. Many claim they want to be a part of a ministry but are not ready. Every leader need to check each person's readiness before sending him out for war. If one is not ready to fight, not only will they be in danger on the battlefield but they will also put others in danger. You see, many Christians want to be a part of God's army but are not ready because their minds need deliverance. God instructed Gideon to bring the remaining men to the water so He could check their minds for battle. The condition of one's mind is very important in choosing a soldier for any army. In the test, they were only concerned about their desire and showed no self-discipline. Again, another 9,700 of the original number failed the test. They rushed into the water, got down on their knees and drank. Also, kneeling down was not a good sign; it show carelessness, impatience, and a lack of self control. Lowering their faces showed that they were not prepared for the sudden attack of an enemy. Clearly, it demonstrated that they were full of themselves and had no discipline. On the other hand, the 300 men who were left demonstrated that they were well prepared for battle. They were not absorbed in themselves, but were well-disciplined and ready for war. During the whole selection process, God rejected 9,700 and chose the 1% (300) of Gideon's recruited army.

Conclusion:

With Gideon's story we can see that when choosing a team or an individual, it is of vital importance to seek God's guidance. Anyone who is afraid to fight the good fight of faith for the Lord should not be selected for leadership in ministry. The possible candidate for the position should exhibit Christ-like character, readiness, bravery, and faith in God. God does not want any one to serve Him against his will. The fearful must go, because courage is vital to soldiery. We see the desirable quality in choosing was their commendable courage to fight in spite of their inadequacy. While the majority says it is impossible, the minority believe nothing is impossible with God. They were also very committed to the cause. When Gideon gathered his army, he sent home all those who were afraid or poorly trained. We need to provide training for those in the ministry who are not trained properly so that they can work in ministry effectively. Only a small army is needed, if God is with it. Many people are looking for large crowds, but quality is more important. Our concern should be in selecting those who would be in the army with us should be those whom God chooses, knowing that it is not about numbers. As long as God is in the army with us is what should really matter.

22

AN ARGUMENT FOR CHRISTIANITY

Although the book of Hebrews was written to the Jewish believers in Jesus, it is an argument for Christianity on a whole. According to Galatians 3:26-29, all believers are one in Christ; there is no longer Jew or Gentile. Christians are reminded that Jesus Christ is the pinnacle of God's revelation to us. It convinces Christians not to give up on their faith. Many people have viewed the prophets, Moses, and even the angels as great, but we learn in Hebrews that Jesus was superior to them. He is our high priest who is making intercession for us. The Mosaic Law was a shadow of Christ. Christ came and fulfilled the law.

The argument of the book of Hebrews was to strengthen the wavering Christians. In order to understand the new covenant we need to understand the old. The writer attributes the faith of the heroes of the Old Testament to how they won God's approval. We do not need to give up our faith because we are no longer under the law but under grace, but we need to continue to hold on unto Jesus who is the author and finisher of our faith. He is the same yesterday, today and forever.

It is a big difference having Christ as a Savior rather than as a priest. Moses was a faithful servant whose example was great to follow, but Jesus Christ is God Himself. All we need is found in Him. Prophets are highly looked upon, but He is greater than any prophet who ever lived. He is far above the angels. He is the creator of angels. Angels bow before him and cry "Holy, Holy, Lord God Almighty."

Jesus replaces the Levites as high priest and His sacrifice is much more efficacious than any Old Testament sacrifice. Those sacrifices couldn't take away sin but Jesus' sacrifice did. Jesus offered himself as a sacrifice without spot or blemish for our sins. The priest alone was able to go before God on people's behalf with sacrifices; this was after they sanctified themselves. We no longer need priests to go to God on our behalf. As long as we have Jesus in our lives, we can go boldly before the throne of grace for ourselves through the blood of Jesus Christ by faith.

23

LAW AND GRACE

The Law of God is of great importance. However, it does not need to be mixed with grace for one to be saved.

The grace of God is all we need to be saved. Grace is an expression of God's goodness. According to the Scripture, grace is God giving to man the exact opposite of what he deserves. You see, we deserve condemnation, instead, by His grace He gives us everlasting life. Ephesians 2:8 says, "For by grace are ye saved through faith." Nowhere in the Scriptures do we see 'for by grace are we saved through the law.' The Scriptures have told us that all we need to do is "believe on the Lord Jesus Christ and thou shalt be saved" (Act 16:31). In this statement, grace has already been established since it is the motive behind salvation.

Although we are not saved by the law but by grace through faith, we need to understand that we cannot live apart from the law. The law contains standards that every believer must live by. The purpose of the law of God is not to save us, but to reveal the nature of God to us and to provide a standard of life for us. If it wasn't for the law, we would not be aware of the sin in our lives. The law reveals that sin is a transgression against God. It reveals the glory of God, how He is holy and how far we miss His standards. Although we are not saved by the law, it is the law of God that is one of the tools God uses to open the eyes of our understanding so that we could come to the knowledge of the truth (1 Tim. 2:4).

Although we are saved by grace, it doesn't mean we are free from the law. In Rom. 6:1, 2, I believe this was a concern why Paul asked the people, "What shall we say then? Shall we continue in sin that grace may abound? God forbid. How shall we that are dead to sin, live any longer in it?" When we are saved by grace, the law opens our eyes to make us aware that our sin nature has died, and it gives us understanding to continue in our new nature without breaking God's law.

Conclusion:

Grace is God's unmerited favor to mankind, while the law is an expression of the will and nature of God. According to "What the Bible is All About," grace cannot begin until the law has proven we are guilty.

24

Will Christ Come Again?

There are enough proofs for us to believe that the return of Christ is sure.

If Jesus was not returning, the Christian's hope would be in vain. We are confident that Jesus is returning because His return is prophesied about all through the Gospel.

The news that Jesus is returning is not from an anonymous, disreputable source but from the source that has never told a lie, the source that cannot lie, the sovereign God. We have the promise of the return of Christ from almost every prophet and writer in the Old Testament. These men did not just write the Word by their own imagination, they were inspired by God. Their prophecies about Christ's first coming came to pass. He came exactly as they said He would come and He will return again just as they said.

While Jesus was on earth, He reassured us of His return. He did not tell us the minute, or the hour, but He told us in Matthew 24 that we will know the season of His coming. The signs of His return that are in Scriptures are evident today. Although we don't know when He will return, He could come back at any moment. Therefore we need to be ready so we can return with Him. He said He was going away to prepare a place for us and would come back to take us with Him (John 14:2-3). Can you imagine how awesome that place is that He is preparing for us? It must be breathtaking. What a blessed hope it is for Christians that Christ will return! Even the angels know that Jesus will return. When Jesus was going back to heaven, the angel of the Lord promised us that Jesus would return.

Conclusion:

All believers are confident of the return of Christ because it was promised by God. His return is the Christian's hope for eternity.

25

LIFE IN THREE TENSES

The life of a Christians has three tenses; the life before salvation, life during salvation, and life after salvation.

In the past tense, we were sinful, wretched and lost without any hope. But God with His love and mercy provided a means of escape for us. He provided us with grace through His Son Jesus Christ. In Christ we have redemption through His blood, the forgiveness of sins. With faith we accept salvation and are declared righteous. The old sinful man is no more, we are now made new with a seal of salvation.

In the present tense, we have received salvation. We are saved from sin and have the power of God, not to walk as we did in the past, but to live in the authority of God, and fulfill the will of God. This cannot be done in our own self but by the Spirit of God that was given to us when we received salvation. We are commissioned to spread the Gospel in this present tense while waiting for the coming of Christ.

In the future tense, there is a blessed hope for all the believers. The Scripture tells us that this time will be the resurrection of all Christians who died in Christ. We who are alive will be caught up to meet Jesus together in the air. We all will be changed from mortality to immortality. We will live in heaven for eternity. No sickness, no more pain, and no death; we will live in joy, peace, and happiness forever. The preaching of the gospel will be over.

Conclusion:

All believers were born in sin and shaped in iniquity. Through Jesus Christ, believers are saved from sin, walk in newness of life, and look forward to an eternal future where there will be joy untold.

26

IN THE TWINKLING OF AN EYE

1 Corinthians 15:51, 52 says, "Behold, I show you a mystery; we shall not all sleep, but we shall all be changed, in a moment, in the twinkling of an eye, at the last trump: for the trumpet shall sound, and the dead shall be raised incorruptible, and we shall be changed."

The Scripture clearly states that like the twinkling of an eye will be the rapture. This is when Christ will return for His Church. It could be at any moment. It is in our best interests that we continue in the faith and live a holy life so that when God returns, we are ready to meet Him. The twinkling of an eye means we will be changed in the time it takes to blink your eye. This is a time of transformation when instantaneously we will put off the old robe of flesh and take on the new robe of Christ. This change will happen so fast that I don't believe we will be able to see the transformation. I believe we will just suddenly experience the new body. It will be time to begin our eternal existence in the presence of the infinite God. God has to do this transformation before we are able to enter into His holy presence. The Bible tells us that flesh and blood cannot inherit the kingdom of heaven.

The reality of Christians being changed in a twinkling of an eye cannot be grasped by the natural mind. This is why the Word of God said this event is a mystery. Believers are able to comprehend it because the Spirit of God enables then. The Spirit of God in believers will also give them insight into the supernatural. It was the Spirit of God who enabled Paul the apostle to see the mysteries in the third heavens.

Conclusion:

When Christ returns, all believers will be changed in the twinkling of an eye. After this event happens, we will reign with Him for eternity.

27

THE DUTY OF SELF-TESTING

Are we who are evangelizing in the faith?

It is very important that we do not rely on other people's diagnosis of our being in the faith. We need to do an accurate examination of ourselves on a regular basis to see whether or not we are in the faith.

Others will give us excellent reports on our Christian walk that will tickle our fancy, only to find out that we are on our way to hell. Going to church and doing all the rituals does not determine our right standing. Receiving good reports from the pastor, deacon, bishop or the overseer does not determine whether we are in the faith. We can be in the church for years and be deceived. We must not think either that because the last time we checked, we were speaking in tongues, healing, preaching or teaching mightily, that we are in the faith.

To be in the faith is much more than getting good reports or doing good works. To be in the faith, our lives must line up with the Word of God. Among the tools that we can use to examine ourselves to see if we are in the faith, is the Word of God. It is the best doctor's manual for self examination. It will reveal side effects of our sin disease, it will tell you what medication you need to cure it, and will give you the steps to prevent it. Prayer is another examination tool. In prayer we can search ourselves, asking God to reveal what is wrong with us, and how we have come short. He will reveal where we came short and at that very moment, we can come into line with Him.

We must identify whether we are in the faith or not; whether or not we think we love God; if we do really love to pray and read the Word of God; do we love the things of God, and do we have the fruit of the Spirit. If we answer "no" to any of these questions, we are not in the faith.

If our desire or first priority is not God, we are giving our service to someone or something else. By doing so, we are in danger; we are left vulnerable to all the enemy's devices. We are also on our way to hell if we are not in the faith.

Conclusion

It doesn't matter if others tell us we are in the faith or even if we believe that we are in the faith. If our lives are not truly lined up with the Word of God, we are wasting our time.

28

CHALLENGES TO HOLY LIVING

All believers are challenged to holy living for many reasons and one of the reasons is because of the coming of the Lord. It is not an option to live a holy life but a requirement.

The Bible says that without holiness it is impossible to see God. For us to see Christ again when He returns we must be holy. The world might not have any clue when the coming of the Lord will be, but Christians are well aware. We were given many clues from Jesus when the season of the Coming of the Lord will be. This time is readily upon us, although we have not been given the day or the hour. It is our responsibility to live a holy life. God could appear any moment without any notice. Therefore, we must not be *getting* ready but *are* ready and waiting to meet Him. Being ready means we are completely yielded to Christ. When we are yielded to Him, we are no longer controlled by sin. God has taken over us, and has caused us to be holy through Christ.

Although Christ is at hand, we should not be sitting comfortably in Zion awaiting His return, but should be productive. Obedience is a part of holy living. God has given us works to do and He is expecting us to be obedient in carrying out the entire task that has been given to us. Carrying out the tasks won't be easy; we have to dress ourselves in holiness for the task to be accomplished. To do this will require great sacrifice. We have to constantly shun sin, study the Word and have a relationship with God, where we seek His face constantly, without ceasing.

Conclusion

Christ is coming back and it is the responsibility of every Christian to live a holy life in order to be ready when He returns.

29

Seven Distinguishing Marks of a Christian

1. **Obedience**: obedience to God, to what He has told you. This is not what we believe but what we do.
2. **Diligence**: be instant in season and out of season. Be diligent in everything you do.
3. **Humility**: be humble. It is not about me, it is about helping other people.
4. **Faithfulness**: it is required of a servant that he is found faithful. Someone once said, "I'd rather see a sermon than read one." We need to show our faithfulness so the world can see it.
5. **Courage**: we should be courageous. Joshua was courageous; Moses was courageous when he went to Pharaoh. We have courage because of who we are in Christ. We have courage because God is with us. Courage and faith go hand in hand.
6. **Devotion**: commitment; we are not our own, we belong to God. In all aspects of our lives we need to be devoted to the Lord.
7. **Uncompromised life**: we must not compromise our calling but maintain our integrity and be **righteous at all times. We are to please God in every thing we do.**

30

Sample Follow-up Plan

There are many people who are doing a great job in the world evangelizing but have no follow up plan in place. I have often heard people say that it is their job to sow and it doesn't matter who reaps the harvest. This statement is so wrong. Why? Because follow up is all a part of the evangelism process. As a matter a fact, it is the most important part. When someone plants a seed, it is very important that he also waters it and makes sure it is rooted in proper soil, and watch it until it is time to be harvested; otherwise, it will be stillborn or the enemy will come and steal the seed out of the heart. Mark 4:14-20 states, "The sower soweth the word. And these are they by the way side, where the word is sown; but when they have heard, Satan cometh immediately, and taketh away the word that was sown in their hearts. And these are they likewise which are sown on stony ground; who, when they have heard the word, immediately receive it with gladness; and have no root in themselves, and so endure but for a time: afterward, when affliction or persecution ariseth for the word's sake, immediately they are offended. And these are they which are sown among thorns; such as hear the word, and the cares of this world, and the deceitfulness of riches, and the lusts of other things entering in, choke the word, and it becometh unfruitful. And these are they which are sown on good ground; such as hear the word, and receive it, and bring forth fruit, some thirtyfold, some sixty, and some an hundred."

Step by step process

Immediate follow-up plan
1. Always provide the person with resources i.e. Pamphlet, evangelism card or Bible, etc. These materials should always have your contact information on them so that the person can contact you.

2. It is also important to obtain contact information from the person you lead to Christ. If possible, obtain a phone number. The person who made the initial contact should call immediately.

3. With contact information it is a good practice to mail a follow up card

Week one

4. Even before you mail a follow up card; it is important that you give the new believer or believers a phone call. The phone call can be from the Deacon or Pastor, etc. at this time. Phone calls should continue every week until the new convert is secure in the congregation.

5. Give an invitation to a new believer to attend church

6. It is necessary that the new believer start drinking newborn milk; therefore, it is necessary that you have a new believer's course in place for all new believers. This can be done at the church or at their home.

Around week four

7. An in-house visit with new believers should take place

Week five

8. Follow up phone call from pastor/leadership team

9. Conduct follow up party where the new believers can get involved and be acknowledged.

10. The above follow up process should continue as needed throughout the months.

11. Team leaders should be assigned to new believers to provide spiritual and physical aid, encouragement, nurturing and love. They should be responsible for briefing and sharing the Gospel of salvation with the new believers. Building a relationship with them, sharing Christ with them and teaching them the basics of the faith are all vital. They should encourage new Christians to be involved in growth events and attend church services. They should phone those under their care; send them messages of encouragement; be sensitive to struggles they experience, and refer them to others who can help when necessary

31

SAMPLE FOLLOW-UP SCRIPT AND LETTERS

Script for Pastors

Hi, my name is _____ and I am the Pastor of _____ Church. Our Evangelism team informed me about your decision to accept Jesus as your Lord and Saviour. We are very excited about your new walk with the Lord and if there is anything our church can do to help you, please do not hesitate to let us know. Would you please provide me with your mailing address so we can send some new believer's materials to assist you as you begin your new life in Christ?
We would also love to have you come and worship with us. We are located at _____ and our service times are from _____ Sundays.

Please be assured that I am praying for you.
Bye for now!

Sample card from bible study team

Hi _____!

We are the Evangelism Team from _____ Church. We want to congratulate you on your decision to make Jesus Christ your Saviour. Our team meets every Wednesday for Bible study and prayer meeting from 7pm to 9pm. We are inviting you to come out and join us.
We have lots of fun together and would love to meet you.
Hope to see you next Wednesday!

Sincerely,
Evangelism God's Way Team.

Sample Leaders/Church Member Phone Script

Hi, my name is _____ and I am calling from_____Church to congratulate you. Our Pastor, _____ shared with me the wonderful news about your decision to accept Jesus as your Lord and Savior. You couldn't make a better choice. If there is any thing we can help you with, please do not hesitate to let us know, the church is here to help you.

Our pastor will be personally mailing you some growth material that will help you in your new life.

Our pastor asked me to confirm your address. Can I verify your address?

Is there anything I can pray about with you before I go?

When you have an opportunity, please feel free to visit with us. We would love to have your presence with us.

We are located at _____. Our service times are _____.

It was a pleasure talking with you. May God bless you in your new walk with Him.

Goodbye!

Follow up script after home visit

Hello! _____. How are you doing? This is _____ From _____ church, who came by the other day. I am just calling to thank you for giving us the opportunity to visit you. Did you get a chance to look over the materials we left? Were they helpful? Do you have any more questions? If there is anything we can do for you, please feel free to let us know. We are looking forward to seeing you again on Sunday.

Bye for now. Have yourself a blessed day!

Sample Letter from Pastor for new converts

3 Markham Rd
Scarborough, ON
M1B 34H

Phone: 416-745-7893
August 27, 2010

Dear John,

It was such a blessing to hear that you have decided to make Jesus Christ your Lord and Saviour. I am indeed filled with joy! You have joined thousands of people who have also accepted Christ. Precious one! You have made one of the best decisions, one that will determine your eternal life. As a new believer, it is very important that you receive good teaching to help you grow, and connect you with those who can help you in your walk. I want to personally invite you to attend our church. Please feel free to contact me if you have any questions. I have included some information to help you in your walk and also our phone number and our church address.

Again, congratulations on your new life with Christ.

God bless you! Hope to see you on Sunday.

Yours in Christ,
Pastor

Community banquet follow-up letter

Church Address
50 Gervais Drive
Toronto, Ontario
M3C 1Z3

Phone: 416-757-3058

Dear _____,

It was a pleasure for _____ to be the host church for the community banquet held on November 27th.

It was a joy to have you join us for this occasion. I trust you enjoyed the dinner and the program put on by the _____.

My prayer is that your introduction to us was a positive one.

If you have any prayer requests, please don't hesitate to contact us.

If you do not have a church home, we invite you to make our church home yours also.

You may want to visit our website at www.xxxxxx.com.

May this Christmas Season bring you and yours the Joy of Christ and may the New Year be the best you have ever had.

Yours in Christ,

_____

Pastor

New Resident in nearby area code (example)

Church Address
2 Morningview Trail
Scarborough, ON

Phone: 416-757-7778

September 3, 2010

Dear Neighbor and Friend,

We are in your Neighborhood! _____Church is associated with ____Worldwide Ministries and has many ministries that help to support families. We presently operate a children and youth program for all ages. We also have a woman's, men's and senior's program to cater to each person's preference.

We would love to have you worship with us some time in the near future. Our Sunday Service conveniently starts at 1:30 pm so that you can sleep in and arrive rested and comfortable.

If you wish to know more about this ministry feel free to contact the number above to speak with our Pastor or a member of our evangelism team.

We are looking forward to meeting you at a time of your convenience. Our prayer team will be praying for you so you can reply with your prayer request.

God bless you and we wish you many blessings in your new home

Yours truly,

Pastor John

New Residents in nearby code (example #2)
By Sharon Atkinson

Church Address

2 Morningview Trail

Scarborough, ON

Phone: 416-757-7778

September 3, 2010

Dear Newcomer:

Greetings, we are pleased to welcome you to _____. The _____ Church in _____ area. We trust that your move was successful, and we are praying that you will be blessed in your new home.

We are inviting you to be a part of our congregation here at _____

We have enclosed a complete schedule of services which are currently available. We have Sunday morning and Friday evening services. Enclosed also is a Evangelism Business card, which can be used to invite your friends or family. We certainly hope that this will be a helpful reminder of our services available. We are also including a schedule for our Bible studies for all ages, including the younger children.

If you have any further information that you need, please feel free to contact us. Or if there is a need for transportation or directions, please do not hesitate to call either W. Molder (Host Pastor) 416-967-7778 or Debbie Colquhoun (Evangelist) at 416-526-0763.

God bless!

Sample letter for Special Event Ticket-Selling, Fund-raising letter
By Sharon Atkinson

Dear John Doe:

We are scheduling our fund-raising concert for November 0, 2010. Last years concert was very successful. We have great expectations for this year. Please remember to highlight this date on your calendar. It will be most definitely memorable.

Deborah Nembhard-Colquhoun

We will have great performances and many artists to enhance your day, granting a great support for our ministry at Evangelism God's Way. This will help us to assist the community who are impoverished, disease stricken, abused or addictions, etc.

We do look forward to your attendance to the upcoming concert November 0, 2010.

Thanking you in advance

Sincerely

Pastor Dee

32

TEACHING OUTLINE FOR BABY CHRISTIANS

What is a teacher? A teacher is one who helps someone else to learn. In other words, the teacher cooperates with the students in learning. He does not seek to perform before an audience made up of listening students, but undertakers with them an activity in which they are busily engaged. There is no teaching unless there is learning. The teacher has not really taught unless the student has learned. The object of our teaching is to make something happen in the life of our student. The test of our teaching is what happens in the life of our student.[22]

Topics:

(1) **Grace and Mercy:** We are saved through God's Grace

1. Rom. 6:23. – "For the wages of sin is death, but the gift of God is eternal life in Christ Jesus our Lord." (All are sinners deserving of death but grace comes to us in our poor sinful condition and offers us the mercy of God when we deserve His wrath). "MERCY" is God withholding the punishment we deserve because of our sinfulness. The consequence of sin is death, yet Jesus paid this penalty for us.

   If it wasn't for God's mercy, you would not be here. We are deserving of judgment, destruction, punishment, and condemnation.

2. Ephesians 2:8 states, "For by grace are ye saved through faith; and that not of yourselves: it is the gift of God." "GRACE" is the unearned gift the Father gives to His children. The Lord relates to us by His grace. Grace has provided salvation to all who come to

---

[22] www.baptistbiblebelievers.com

Him, even though we deserved destruction. God knew that the man He created would sin.

3. Psalms 111:4 says, "He hath made his wonderful works to be remembered: the LORD is gracious and full of compassion."
4. Psalm 136 says, "His mercy endureth forever."
5. 2 Corinthians 12:9 states, "My grace is sufficient for thee: for my strength is made perfect in weakness."
6. Romans 3:24 says, "Being justified freely by his grace through the redemption that is in Christ Jesus."
7. Titus 3:7 says, "That being justified by his grace, we should be made heirs according to the hope of eternal life."

(2) **Love: You are loved by God**

1. John 3:16 says, "For God so loved the world, that he gave his only begotten Son, that whosoever believeth in him should not perish, but have everlasting life
2. Romans 5:8 says, "But God commendeth his love toward us, in that, while we were yet sinners, Christ died for us."
3. 1 John 3:1; "Behold, what manner of love the Father hath bestowed upon us, that we should be called the sons of God: therefore the world knoweth us not, because it knew him not."
4. 1 John 4:9-10; "In this the love of God was made manifest among us, that God sent his only Son into the world, so that we might live through him. In this is love, not that we have loved God but that he loved us and sent his Son to be the propitiation for our sins."
5. 1 John 4:12; "No man hath seen God at any time. If we love one another, God dwelleth in us, and his love is perfected in us."
6. 1 John 4:13; "And we have seen and do testify that the Father sent the Son to be the Saviour of the world."

(3) **Forgiveness: You are forgiven of your sins by God through Jesus Christ**

1. 1 John 1:9; "If we confess our sins, he is faithful and just to forgive us our sins and to cleanse us from all unrighteousness."

2. Daniel 9:9; "To the Lord our God belong mercy and forgiveness, though we have rebelled against him."
3. Matthew 26:28; "for this is my blood of the covenant, which is poured out for many for the forgiveness of sins."
4. Mark 1: 4, "John did baptize in the wilderness, and preach the baptism of repentance for the remission of sins."
5. Luke 24:47, "And that repentance and remission of sins should be preached in his name among all nations, beginning at Jerusalem."
6. Acts 2: 38, "Then Peter said unto them, Repent, and be baptized every one of you in the name of Jesus Christ for the remission of sins, and ye shall receive the gift of the Holy Ghost."
7. Acts 26:18, "To open their eyes, and to turn them from darkness to light, and from the power of Satan unto God, that they may receive forgiveness of sins, and inheritance among them which are sanctified by faith that is in me."
8. Ephesian1:7, "In whom we have redemption through his blood, the forgiveness of sins, according to the riches of his grace."

(4) Baptism: What is the significance of Baptism?

1. **John 3:36** says: "He that believeth on the Son hath everlasting life: and he that believeth not the Son shall not see life; but the wrath of God abideth on him."
2. **John 5:24** says: "Verily, verily, I say unto you, He that heareth my word, and believeth on him that sent me, hath everlasting life, and shall not come into condemnation: but is passed from death unto life." The Scriptures tell us that we believe first and then we are baptized. Baptism does not save anyone.
3. **In Acts 2:38:** What does "baptized for remission of sins" mean? It means union with Jesus. The Apostle Paul speaks of "being united with Him" by baptism (Romans 6:5): "All of you who were baptized into Christ have put on Christ," "Then Peter said unto them, Repent, and be baptized every one of you in the name of Jesus Christ for the remission of sins, and ye shall receive the gift of the Holy Ghost."
4. **Romans 6:3-4; Colossians 2:12,** The Bible also refers to baptism as a symbol of dying to the old life and burying it when the

believer goes down under the water. When he or she comes up out of the water after baptism, the Bible likens it to rising from the grave with Christ to a new life.

5. **Acts 22:16,** "And now why are you waiting? Arise and be baptized, and wash away your sins, calling on the name of the Lord."

6. **Romans 6:1-4**, Baptism is an outward sign of an inward commitment. Water baptism is our way of showing what has happened inside our hearts.

7. **I Corinthians 12:13,** "For by one Spirit are we all baptized into one body, whether we be Jews or Gentiles, whether we be bond or free; and have been all made to drink into one Spirit."

(5) Prayer: Jesus' Model Prayer for Believers

(1) Matthew 5-9, **how to and how not to pray**-those who pray with wrong motives will receive their rewards and likewise those who pray with right motives will receive also their rewards.

(2) Matthew 6:9, **To whom we should pray to:** Jesus said, "Our Father." God is the Father in that He is the Creator of all mankind (Gen. 1, 2). He is also a caring Father who provides both physically and spiritually (Matt. 5:45; 6:33). We have access to our heavenly Father, we are not praying to a natural father but a supernatural father, a divine father, an everlasting father. He is Father of us all.

(3) **Matthew 6:9, How to approach God in Prayer**: "Hallowed be thy name" He is a holy God, when we go before Him, we should not go just any way we choose. We need to respect him, reverence Him, and honour Him; this is a time to give Him the praises He deserves; this is also a time to repent of our sins before Him.

(4) **Matthew 6:11, What we should ask for in prayer**: "Give us this day our daily bread." We might be at the bottom of our resources and have no one to help us but God will provide for us if we ask him. "Bread" in this passage is not referring to the things we want in life but the things that we need. (Matt. 4: 4). Jesus taught us to take life one day at a time. Many problems can be solved if we focus on "today," nor last week, not yesterday, or tomorrow. Through prayer we can ask for our daily needs and He will supply all our needs according to His riches…

(5) Matthew 6:12, Forgiveness through prayer: Jesus said, "And forgive us our debts…" All are sinners, even Christians (Rom. 3:23, I Jn. 1:8-10). No matter how bad our sins are, in prayer we can ask God to forgive us of all our sins. Confession of sin is required (I Jn. 1:7). There are, indeed, conditions to receiving forgiveness. We must ask in faith, ask unselfishly, and ask in a state of obedience (Jas. 1:6; Jas. I Jn. 3:22). Another condition is, "as we forgive our debtors." Jesus explained, "But if ye forgive not men their trespasses, neither will your Father forgive your trespasses" (Matthew 6: 15).

(6) <u>Matthew 6:13, Praying about temptation:</u> We are faced with temptation everyday, but if we ask God in prayer, He will lead us into all truth; God has promised that His children will be provided a way of escape.

(6) Healing: We can receive healing through Jesus Christ

1. <u>Isaiah 53:5</u>, "But he was wounded for our transgressions, he was bruised for our iniquities: the chastisement of our peace was upon him; and with his stripes we are healed."

2. **1 Peter 2:24,** "Who his own self bare our sins in his own body on the tree, that we, being dead to sins, should live unto righteousness: by whose stripes ye were healed." Note: Jesus died for both our sins and our sicknesses. Our healing is in Jesus Christ through his atonement sacrifice. **We are already healed.**

3. **Matthew 4:23-24** "And Jesus went about all Galilee, teaching in their synagogues, and preaching the gospel of the kingdom, and healing all manner of sickness and all manner of disease among the people. And his fame went throughout all Syria: and they brought unto him all sick people that were taken with divers diseases and torments, and those which were possessed with devils, and those which were lunatick, and those that had the palsy; and he healed them." Note: Jesus has power to heal "every disease and sickness." There are no limits to healing.

4. **John 4:49-51** "The nobleman saith unto him, Sir, come down ere my child die. Jesus saith unto him, Go thy way; thy son liveth. And the man believed the word that Jesus had spoken unto him, and he went his way. And as he was now going down, his servants met him, and told him, saying, Thy son liveth."

5. **James 5:14** "Is any sick among you? let him call for the elders of the church; and let them pray over him, anointing him with oil in the name of the Lord."

6. Notes: healing is ministered to people: people can be healed through the spoken word. They can also be healed through the laying on of hands, prayer, and anointing of oil by the elders.

33

CHARACTERISTICS TO FINISH WELL

2 Timothy 4:6-21

- When faced with trials and suffering, continue to persevere for the Lord. Persistence in difficult times and discipline is important for our race to the finish line.
- We need perspective that will enable us to focus.
- We should maintain a positive attitude at all times.
- We should manifest Christ-like character by living by the fruit of the Spirit.
- Truth must be lived out in our lives so that convictions and promises of God are seen to be real.
- We need to maintain a continual, meaningful, personal relationship with others with whom we are associated to, and especially with God.
- Intimacy with Christ is important.
- Be faithful to others and God and invest in the lives of others on an ongoing basis.
- Live the Christian walk with expectancy (expectation of a reward is a good motivating factor).
- It is very difficult to live this Christian walk without faith; therefore, we need faith in God.
- Engage in spiritual disciplines such as prayer, fellowship, study, worship, and fasting.
- A humble and obedient spirit is important.
- Have healthy relationships with resourceful people.

- Be Spirit-filled, so that God will strengthen and equip us to carry out His calling on our lives.
- When faced with loneliness, take courage, knowing that God will never leave you.

34

CHRISTIAN JOY

Christ is the only source of the Christian's joy. If we are in Christ, we must have joy at all times. Joy should be in our living, in our service, and even in tribulation.

Philippians 1:21 says, "for to me to live is Christ." If Christ is in us we have no choice but to manifest joy, because we are no longer controlled by the sinful nature but by the Spirit of God. Phil. 4:4 says, "Rejoice in the Lord always: and again I say, Rejoice!" Once we are in Christ, our aim and purpose is to glorify God in everything we do. We cannot truly glorify God without joy. Joy is one of the fruit of the Spirit. In John 15 we are told that in order to produce the fruit of the Spirit we must abide in the vine, which is Christ Jesus. We abide in Christ by reading the Word of God, spending time with Him in prayer, praising Him, witnessing about Him, doing good works, fleeing from sin, etc. As we abide in Christ, His life and power flows into us through the Holy Spirit.

Once we are living in the will of God, we will experience great joy, regardless of our circumstances. Once a Christian is rooted in Christ, he or she can rejoice in tribulation like the apostle Paul. Paul went through great tribulation and was able to maintain joy. This is because Paul knew in whom he believed and was anchored in Christ completely. It is not easy to rejoice in an atmosphere that is gloomy, but the joy of the Lord is our strength; in a weary land, the joy of the Lord is a supernatural joy that will change any atmosphere. It doesn't matter the environment we find ourselves in, the joy of the Lord in us should be unchanged.

Jesus came with joy not to be served, but to serve. We are also to follow His footsteps. We are not to serve with complaints or grouchiness. It is impossible to do a good service if it is not joyful. God has given us joy so we can be at peace with ourselves and also so we can extend it to others in whatever service we might render to others. The joy of the Spirit is not a fruit to keep hidden or allowed to rot, but is to be displayed and shared. Our service to God and to others should be joyful; otherwise it will not be effective. God loves a cheerful server. We will find fulfillment in joyful service, and we will receive eternal rewards from God.

Conclusion

God will not accept dead sacrifices; therefore, we must go before Him with a joyful heart. We miss all the benefits when our offerings are not accepted, but when our offerings are accepted, all the treasures of heaven are open to us.

35

GOD'S MISSIONARY CALL

Mission is God's will for His people, mission is nothing new, it began in the Old Testament and continues today. The missionary purpose of God is all throughout the Scriptures. In Scripture we read of God's calling upon Abraham to go on a missionary journey. Much blessing was attached to this call. God sometimes calls us into ministry like he did Abraham and through such ministry He will give us great promises that will come to pass. However, we must step out in faith. Abraham had no clue where he was going, yet he left everything behind and followed God's calling upon his life.

The same God who chose and called Abraham into missions is the same God who is choosing us today. In the choosing of Abraham, we read of God's promises and we also read of the promises being fulfilled. God did not go back on His promises to Abraham and He will not go back on His promises to us today. He is a faithful God who never disappoints. His Word says that He honours His words above His very name.

God might have whispered some impossible promises in your spirit: for instance: He is going to bless you with a signs and wonders ministry so that the nation will be drawn to Him…If we utter some of these promises, people would think that we were losing our minds. Let's hold on to these promises, knowing that we serve a mighty God, the God of the impossible. We need to take courage that God promised Abraham the impossible and it came to pass. One of the promises was that Abraham's descendants were going to be as numerous as the stars and the sand on the sea shore. Keep in mind that his wife was way past the years of child bearing, not to mention she was barren. Abraham himself was too old, also. Note the key to God's fulfilled promise: Abraham believed the Lord. Do you believe the Lord? Do you believe that even on our missionary journey evangelizing God will cause a nation to be blessed through us? Yes, He can! As a matter of fact, this promise was already promised in Scriptures. All we have to do is obey God as Abraham did and He will cause it to come to pass. The harvest is ready but the labourers are few. Let us be labourers so that God's promise of a large harvest (souls) can be fulfilled. Abraham's wife was barren and God through His mighty Spirit allowed life to come to her womb and she conceived. Out of that conception came the nation of Israel and the spiritual Israel the (church), through Jesus Christ. Sometimes it may appear as though nothing is happening or nothing can possibly happen through the ministry God has called us to, but let's take what He did in Abraham's life and apply it to ours. God is able to do great and mighty things, things that we could never comprehend. Today there might be a drought, but tomorrow there will be showers of rain, so much rain that we will not have enough containers to hold the volume of it. The results of such rain will cause numberless sprouts to bud and eventually turn into a great harvest.

The blessing of Abraham has been passed down to us through Jesus Christ. Part of this blessing is salvation through Jesus Christ and we are in God's plan to bring His people into the fold so they too can be partakers of such blessing.

36

ANTICIPATING A GREAT HARVEST

With the condition of the world today we see very little hope of a worldwide revival. However, despite what we are able to see, we can place ourselves in expectation of a revival because of several truths: revival came out of such conditions numerous times in the past, Jesus also promises revival and the Holy Spirit will accomplish revival.

Because the prince of the world is active in influencing people, there is a spiritual barrenness in most parts of the world. This trend is nothing new; it can be dated all the way back to before Jesus came. The good thing though, is that this trend was broken on the day of Pentecost by the indwelling of the Holy Spirit. The same Spirit that caused such a mighty revival continues throughout the centuries and is still capable today of reviving mankind's spiritual barrenness.

Jesus knew that such a time like this would come. He taught in the Scriptures that evil would multiply and people would also multiply across the earth (Matt. 24). No wonder He also promised that in these very last days He would pour out His Spirit on all flesh. This is the time! There is a supernatural solution for revival and it is found in none other than the same Holy Spirit who started the work at the beginning of the church and it is the same mighty Holy Spirit who is about to overflow this land and bring about one of the mightiest revivals the world has ever seen.

When we compare "the growth of the church today is on a scale that is unique in the history to the world."[23] Putting together the different Christian denominations, even those who call themselves Christians by name only, we see that the number of churches (the body of Christ) today have come up to the highest on the scale in this century. Despite these

---

23 Patrick Johnstone, Prespectives on the World Christian Movement, Forth Edition Published 2009. USA p. 383

findings and the many evangelistic efforts, many have heard the Gospel and still have not yet accepted Christ as their Saviour. There are also many who still have not yet heard the Gospel. With this trend, not only is there a great need for revival among Christians, but there is also still a great need for souls. There has never been a greater time to be involved in evangelism than today. The harvest is truly plenteous, the evil is at its climax, and the Holy Spirit is ready to be poured out on all flesh.

There have been times of spiritual barrenness throughout history. God then stepped in with an outpouring of His Holy Spirit, thus bringing revival. This was on a local, national and even regional level. Today not only is He able, He is also ready and willing. Let us evangelize the nations so we can be a part of God's plan.

37

THE HOLY SPIRIT'S WORK IN A COMMUNITY

For the unbeliever to come to be saved, he or she must first understand God's moral rules and also understand that they are in violation of them. Although God's moral standards are set, the community is not always in line with them. Some standards are practiced by the community and this is not intentional. How an individual understands God's rules sometimes is based on their culture. Man cannot desire their own moral rules; the Word of God is the only means by which man can know the moral rules of God. This is where the Evangelist comes in, to take the Word of God throughout the community. The work of the evangelist in getting people to the level of complete understanding of God's moral rules is usually a process. This is partly because of the many different factors that are associated with each ethnicity within a community, their different practices and beliefs. Mankind thinks in his own eyes that he is doing good.

Evangelists must understand that man does not have consciousness in himself of God's rules, therefore cannot decide their own moral rules. It is their responsibility to bring the Word to the community. However, it is only the work of the Holy Spirit, as the Word does the work of conviction, who opens their understanding, and gives them consciousness of God's moral law. It is also by the Holy Spirit that God leads individuals through the transformation process, within a community.

Apart from understanding the process of acceptance and transformation, the evangelist should learn the different cultural and ethical systems so they can know how to overcome obstacles and wrong accusations about God. Though faced with opposition while evangelizing a community, we can rest assured, knowing that the Holy Spirit is at work through us, through His Word, and in the lives of individuals, thus changing their lives.

Another Perspective

The unbeliever must have a strong conviction by the Holy Spirit to recognize and admit they have sinned against the rules of God. This conviction is the first step in ones walk with the Lord. It brings the individual to a place of repentance and puts us on the road to sanctification; a real relationship with God will now be established.

We must however be careful not to confuse the Commandments or rules of God with traditions and culture. The Word of God clearly establishes God's will and direction for the believer. Culture cannot take priority when we seek to please God because man cannot design their own rules. We would find ourselves in opposition of God if we were to design our own rules and this would have devastating consequences. This is why the work of the Evangelist is so important and urgent. There duty is to get believers at a level of complete understanding of God's Word.

38

EVANGELIST COVERING THE EARTH

Although the world-wide spread of the Gospel appears complete, there are still many parts of this world that have not yet heard the Gospel. Challenging factors are: geographical, ethnic, and urban challenges. For us to reach the unreached areas we need to first know where they are and also their beliefs.

According to Patrick Johnstone, Director of Recherch for WEC international, some unreached countries are: Kingdom of Mustang on Nepal's Northern border, Maldive Island in the Indian Ocean, Congo jungles where the Pygmy people live, parts of Central Asia and Mecca where Christians are not allowed The unreached are not only at these places, they are all over the world. There are still a high percentage of the Muslim, Hindu and Buddhist cultures that have not yet heard the Gospel. This is within and within their country of origin. Many have migrated to other parts of the world, even where the Gospel is available and still haven't been reached. Among some of these cultures the height of evil is at its peak. This is because the practice of Satan is dominant. The works of darkness have yet to be broken down.

There is no doubt that there are many all over the world serving as missionaries and evangelists; however, that in itself is not enough. It is necessary that each representative of Christ have the true Christ in him or her.

Despite the challenges, Christ has a vast opportunity to reach the unreached people with the Gospel... Today we have the Bible translated into almost every language; we have literature/material also available in almost every language. We also have a variety of audio-video messages for a "multitude of languages and dialects available to viewers". Human effort has been very effective throughout the centuries in taking the Gospel around the world. However, the spreading of the Gospel will soon be widespread and this is partly because of the advancement in technology. For instance, radio, satellite, TV, and computer etc. will all be widely used. With these means, humans still will have to play a part by taking the Gospel into all the world. These sources are only an aid but not complete on their own. Let's not forget the urban challenges. For example: church planting requires people. We are living in a time where secularism is at its peak: we find that everywhere in the world sin is more acceptable than righteousness, people are preoccupied in gaining wealth, fame...this is an area that also needs to be evangelized but sadly, in most cases it is neglected because the focus of most missionaries is in the rural countryside rather than the urban cities.

39

EVANGELISM LEADERS RESPONSIBILITIES: A & B

Work with evangelism board and coordinator to coordinate all aspects of evangelistic activities.

Participates in and directs outreach activities, weekly visitation, witnessing, and ministry.

Work with evangelism board and coordinator to establish plans for effective evangelism.

Work with evangelism board to plan training seminars, workshops, crusades, evangelistic events and programs for training members in effective evangelism.

Assess, lead and encourage other leaders and members in their evangelism efforts.

Live the Gospel at all times.

Disciple others, and at all times conduct yourself in a way that honours God.

Seek to encourage members of the church to participate in evangelism and motivate then in winning the unsaved to Christ.

Make friends by encouraging and supporting growing believers. Extend love and compassion to them.

Should encourage young Christians to be involved in growth events and attend church services.

Keep and update the records, which include contact information of every person evangelized.

Pray daily for souls to be saved and pray for everyone within the group and all other ministries that you are working with. Should attend corporate prayer opportunities provided through ministry.

Be involved in fellowship, express love at all times to other believers.

Be involved in personal evangelism by making contact with unsaved, building relationships with them, sharing Christ with them, and following up with them in the basics of the faith.

Leaders must actively be involved in the ministry of discipleship. They should also engage in mentoring at least one person within the group by meeting together with them on a regular basis to help them grow spiritually.

Leaders are expected to establish contact with their care group, both inside and outside of group meetings. They should phone those under their care; send them messages of encouragement; be sensitive to struggles they experience, and refer them to others who can help where necessary.

Leaders should exercise their spiritual gifts appropriately.

Leaders must conduct follow up of new believers and also oversee other leaders who are assigned to them and make sure that they are carrying through with the follow up plan also.

Leaders Responsibilities: B

a) Attend evangelism training and meetings
b) Participate in evangelism functions/events that the evangelism team will be planning
c) Attend professional workshops
d) Evangelize
e) Lead
f) Organize
g) Discipleship
h) Teach

i) **Follow up**
- After thorough training, each leader will be assigned a team from the congregation or new members
- They are to schedule a meeting with each person
- Go over with their team the material that will be provided
- Provide brief training to team
- Schedule time to go out and evangelize with team
- Follow up with those who provide contact information
- Report to coordinator on concerns, contact, guidance, suggestions etc.

Please Note: You are the leader of your team; therefore, don't be afraid to be creative, use the information that I will be providing and never forget to include God in the role of winning souls for the kingdom of God.

40

Sample Ministry Plan

Contact Information:
Name: Deborah Nembhard or Yvonne Harvot
Address: 50 Gerrard Dr, Toronto, ON
L1M 4E8

Phone: 905-619-0000

Name of Ministry: Evangelism God's Way

Logo: **EGW**

Executive Summary

VISION and GOALS

-To prepare God's people in spreading the Gospel of Jesus Christ to the world. This will be done through preaching, teaching, counseling and leading. The main activities our ministry includes: Effectively equipping leaders in established ministry, and training Christian workers who have a common belief in the Gospel of Jesus Christ.

We conduct national and international conferences, workshops, tent meetings, and evangelistic crusades. In addition, this ministry reaches the lost by going door to door, ministering on the streets, in hospitals, prisons, and anywhere else needed. As the ministry grows we will support abused women, widows, seniors, and homeless centres with finances and spiritual training both nationally and internationally.

Objectives: How are we going to make a difference?
- Without hesitation, we are prepared to rescue those that are perishing by stepping in and helping by whatever means necessary
- We help Christians create new opportunities to share Christ in their daily lives
- Provide up to date evangelism training to leaders and members
- Encourage them by sharing relevant information and life-changing testimonies
- Providing believers with adequate evangelistic resources
- Identify gifts in individuals and utilize them in evangelism teams
- Raise up leaders to facilitate Outreach Teams
- Develop and implement follow up and Discipleship Programs

Ministry Profile

Evangelism God's Way Team will start out as a simple proprietary ministry, owned by its founder, _____. As the Ministry grows, I will consider re-registering as a limited liability Ministry or as a corporation, whichever will better suit the future Ministry needs. Evangelism God's Way is a home based ministry located in _____. Administration office would always do outreach.

Strategic Alliances / Professional Advisors:

We will make conscious efforts to align ourselves with individuals and organizations that encompass a vast range of spiritual knowledge, resources…that we will make available to our client base. We will also align ourselves with professional advisors who will assist us in this project.

1. Example: Dr. Thomas
2. Coach: Pastor Brown
3. Director of Evangelism
4. Establish Evangelists in different countries including Canada

Church Analysis/Research
- Church growth is reported to be at a rate of 2%.
- The Church (the body of Christ) is at ease in Zion.

- Most Churches have no idea that all believers are called to evangelize.
- Some believers are interested in starting an evangelism ministry, but have no idea where to start.
- The Church (the body of Christ) has lost its zeal to witness for Christ and its fervent love for others.
- There are no evangelism strategies in place for outreach in most Churches.
- A low percentage of the Church (the body of Christ) have some sort of evangelism going on but no discipleship or follow up plan in place.

SWOT Analysis

Competitor	Strength	Weakness	Opportunity for you	Threats by them
Jehovah's Witness	They have a strong team of experienced committed leaders	They offer no real fulfillment	Provide the true Gospel with lasting satisfaction	We have very little time to contribute
Mormons	Well established, Missionaries are committed and confident	They provide false hope	Provide the pure Gospel, hope, and real love	Low budget for paying missionaries
Muslims	Their buildings are modern, huge and flexible	They don't integrate the women into mass worship. lack modern music resources	Provide the life changing Gospel to them	Lack of resources and manpower

Marketing Plan

For the Ministry to grow we will use the following advertising tools: business cards, pamphlets, letters to churches, revival tents, web sites, face book, local papers, and posters on bulleting boards etc.

We will focus our efforts in the following market segment:

1. Churches—meet pastors with proposals
2. Religious organizations
3. Unbelievers
4. Homeless
5. Street
6. Conduct missions in poor countries

Church Proposal

Organize a team of leaders from each congregation. Provide them with training. This will include practical and biblical training:

1. -hands on experience (go out with each member on the field) door-to-door, hospital etc
2. -involve them in workshops, conferences, etc
3. -direct and assist them in planning evangelism events
4. -teach them the discipleship process and follow up process
5. -create tools to keep them motivated

Evangelism Leaders Responsibilities

1. Attend evangelism training and meeting
2. Participate in evangelism functions/events that the evangelism team will be planning
3. Attend professional workshops
4. Evangelize
5. Lead
6. Organize
7. Discipleship
8. Teach

9. Pray
10. Follow up

Resources

<u>Provide each leader of each team with evangelism materials: We have put together an evangelism kit which includes:</u>

Teaching booklets and CD's on evangelism:

1. The Importance of Evangelism
2. Why Evangelize
3. The Pre-requisites for Evangelism
4. Different Styles of Evangelism

The kit also includes: Bibles, tracts, evangelism business cards, short CD's of the Gospel, sample letters for follow up/donations, invitations, follow up cards and more.

After these leaders are fully trained they would continue the same process with members from the congregation who have the desire to evangelize.

We will also conduct conferences/workshops to encourage the entire church to participate in evangelism.

We will also present a panel from our evangelism ministry who would share their testimony/experiences in evangelism which includes: positive and negative encounters, opposition, challenges and fulfillments, etc.

This church project will be free of charge, although donations are accepted.

<u>Training Agenda:</u>

There will be sessions every Saturday from January to the end of March. These sessions will give all leaders an evangelistic overview. Every Saturday we will be covering different topics on evangelism and also going out into the harvest field to witness.

Starting in April, we will be commencing our training sessions with other leaders from different congregations. The leaders from Evangelism

Gods Way Team/TCC Evangelism team will be responsible to do the teaching/training on a rotation basis. We are currently working with three churches. However; there is a need for more marketing in order to have a good start for April.

In addition to the training sessions that will be starting in April at Canada Christian College, we will also be conducting a New Believer's Course. Most students are expected to come from our weekly witnessing.

Meeting

At the end of the Evangelism overview sessions, we will be conducting a general meeting with board members, leaders and members of the Evangelism team to discuss organizational plans, responsibilities and procedures etc. Example, meeting agenda per category:

- After thorough training, each leader will be assigned a team
- They are to schedule a meeting with their team
- Go over the materials that will be provided with their team
- Provide brief training with team
- Schedule time to go out and evangelize with team *(leaders that are not from TCC do not have to participate, however are welcome to participate if desired)*
- Follow up with those who provide contact information
- Report to Director on concerns, contacts, guidance, suggestions etc.

Financial Plan

Sponsors/donations, special events etc. We will be meeting with institutions that can fund us. We will print, publish, sell and distribute Christian literature, make videos, and CD's. Will collect, solicit and accept funds under the Canadian Revenue Agency, Taxation guidelines or other subscriptions for carrying on the work…

Suggested Treasurer for this ministry—John Doe

Bank account to be set up—

Start-up Expenses

I estimate that the start-up costs will be $410 (including, logo design, advertising, Materials). The start-up costs are to be financed by generated profit from the first function and a portion from _____ personal funds (i.e., donation of around a total of $200).

Business cards $60

Brochure $150

Evangelism kit $150

Advertisement $50 or we could seek free advertisement

Future Plan

-near future plans for board: salaries, benefits, insurance and incentives

-purchase material for project

-conduct ongoing training for leaders

-create website

-TV broadcasting/advertisement

-office for the ministry

-join networking group

-hire an accountant

-expound internationally

- have your own vehicle

-counseling team

-nutritional advisor

-prayer line

-musician team

-praise team

-preaching team

-teaching team

[One person each to be selected from executive board to direct each team]

Our keys to success:

1. Allowing God to lead and direct us, pray, pray, pray
2. Love, unity and respect for each other
3. Maintain a professional image
4. Hard work, perseverance and commitment

Organization Chart

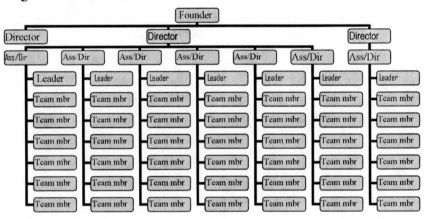

Start up Customer List and Phone

Name of Church	Number of Team Leaders	Phone Number
RT Tabernacle	10	416-226-0991

Deborah Nembhard-Colquhoun

Training Schedule / Evangelism / visitation-for Team

DATE	TRAINING TIME	EVANGILISM practice	DEBRIEFING	VISITATION
Saturday	Eg. 11am-11:30 With evang. Shaw	12-1:00pm With Evan. Mack	1:30-2:00pm With team	home
Saturday	With Evang. Brown			hospital
Saturday				Event planning
Saturday				Street etc.

41

Sample Evangelism Forms & Schedules

Team Leader Phone List / Address

Name	Address	Phone Number

Event schedule

	Date	Location	Detail
Prayer [3 times per month]			
Board Meeting			
Leaders meeting			
Fundraising Event			
Brochure completion			
Proposal to churches			
Proposal to church			
Welcome wagon delivery			
Holiday outreach			Christmas, Easter
Hospital Visitation			
Door to door outreach			
Prison outreach			
Airport outreach			
Free community dinner			
Conference			Example: Youth Evangelism Explosion
International mission			

Evangelism God's Way Manual

Evangelism Schedule

January 2011– March 2011

DATE	TIME	ADGENDA	LEADERS ROTATION	Topics:
Jan. 21-March 2011 Every Saturday Date for each Leader to be assigned	11-12pm	Prayer > >	Names:	-revival -souls -the team -unity/love -perseverance -direction -miracle/healing -etc
				Training Topics:
Jan-March 211 Every Saturday	12-12:30pm	Training > >	Names:	-Office of the Evangelist -Evangelism Overview -Why evangelize? -How to reach different religion/ testimonial-msg -The follow up plan -New Believers overview -Different style of Evangelism -Evangelism Overview
Every Saturday	12:30-1:30pm	Evangelism >	**Names:**	-door-to-door -street -hospital -nursing home -prison
General Meeting	March	Organizational plan-moving fwd		

March 2011-December 2011

DATE	TIME	ADGENDA	LEADERS ROTATION	
March 2011-Dec.2011 Every Saturday Date for each Leader to be assigned	11-12pm	Prayer >	Names	
				Training Topics:
March-December Every Saturday Date for each teacher to be assigned	12-12:30pm 20min for teaching 10 min for testimonial msg	Training >	Names	-Evangelism Overview -Office of the Evangelist -Different style of Evangelism -The follow up plan -Testimonial-message -How to reach different religion -New Believers overview
Every Saturday	12:00- 12:30	Hands on Training >	Names	
Every Saturday	12:30- 1:30pm	New Believers > Course	Names	
June18/11	EVANGELISM SERVICE	involver to assigned		
7pm	Worship Sermon Testimonial-Message Alter call			

Evangelism God's Way Manual

July 1/11	Evangelism party in the park- agenda to reach the lost			
July 14/11	Free Community BBQ			
August 22/11	International Mission			
August 13/11	Concert to raise funds for mission			
Oct. 8/11	Evang. Dinner/Concert			
Nov. 19/11	Evangelism Service			
	Worship Sermon Testimonial- Message Alter call			

Date: _____

EVANGELISM SIGN UP SHEET

NAME	PHONE NUMBER	E-MAIL ADDRESS

42

Sample Evangelism Questioner

Evangelism Questionnaire 1
1. What do you think is the greatest need in the world?
Peace
Love
Other

2. What is the most important thing in your life?
Family
Friend
Job/Money
Religion
Other

3. Where or to whom would you go if you had spiritual questions?
Friends
Parents
Pastor/Priest
Bible
Other

4. What do you think of Jesus?
Good Man
Myth
Son of God
Other

Don't Know
5. Do you think it is possible to know God personally?
Yes
No
Don't Know
6. Have you come to the place in your spiritual life where you are certain that if you died tonight you would go to heaven?
Yes
Hope So
No
7. If you stood before God and He asked you, "Why should I let you into my heaven?" what would you answer?
Lived a good life
Don't know
I believe
Jesus died for me
Other

Evangelism God's Way Manual

Religious Questionnaire 2 (Part 1)
Are you the member of any religious group?
Yes
No
Used to be
Joining
2. What religious group is this? If not, were you brought up in the beliefs of a religious group?
Christian
Islam
Hindu
Individual
Other_____ _____ _____ _____

3. Where you brought up in this religion? If not, skip.
Yes
No
4. At what period of your life did you become interested in this religion? If not, at what period did you become disinterested?
Childhood
Adolescence
Early adulthood
Middle life
Later life
5. Do you ever participate in religious services?
Yes
No
6. How often do you participate in religious services?
Daily
Weekly
Monthly
Annually
7. How far do you travel to these religious services?
1-5 miles
5-10 miles
10-20 miles
20 or more miles
8. If you had children, would you rear them in this religion?
Yes
No
Other_____ _____ _____ _____
_____ _____ _____ _____

Religious Questionnaire 2 (Part 2)

9. To what religious writings do you adhere to, if any?
Bible_____
Koran_____
Torah_____
Other_____

10. How often do you refer to this religious book?
Daily_____
Weekly_____
Monthly_____
Annually_____

11. How do your religious beliefs influence the way you live?
In every way_____
In most things_____
In some things_____
Very little_____
Not at all_____

12. Do you seek to tell your acquaintances about your religious beliefs?
Never_____
Seldom_____
Sometimes_____
Regularly_____

13. Do you feel that your religion is the only true religion?
Yes_____
No_____

14. Are you certain that if you died tonight you would achieve "salvation" in your religion?
Yes_____
Hope so_____
No_____

15. If you stood before the Supreme Being and He asked you, "Why should I let you into my heaven?" what would you answer?
Lived a good life_____
Did my best_____
Don't know_____
I believe_____
Other_____

16. Can I show you a pamphlet which may assist you in your religious journey?
Yes_____
No_____

Those not wanting to complete questionnaire_____

Evangelism God's Way Manual

Neighborhood Questionnaire I

Initials of Surveyors: _____

Date: _____

Address: _____

Name (if known): _____

1. According to you, what is the greatest need in this community?

2. What advice do you have for a church here in this community?

3. How can we as a local church help you?

Immediate Evaluation

Needs expressed: ☐ Spiritual; ☐ Material; ☐ Psychological; ☐ Other:
_____

Did you speak about: ☐ God? ☐ Gospel? ☐ Bible study? ☐ Other?
_____

Spiritual Response: ☐ Open; ☐ Closed; ☐ Other:
_____

Would another contact be worthwhile? ☐ Yes; ☐ No; ☐ Other:

Neighborhood Questionnaire II

Initials of Surveyors: _____

Date: _____

Address: _____

Name (if known): _____

1. Do you think people attend church now as often as they did 10 years ago?

2. Why do you think people attend church these days?

3. To what age group do you think the church should be giving more attention?

4. Have you come to the place in your spiritual life where you are certain that if you died tonight you would go to heaven?
   - ❏ Yes; ❏ No.
   - ❏ Other: _____

5. If you stood before God and He asked you, "Why should I let you into my heaven?" what would you answer?

Immediate Evaluation

Needs expressed: ❏ Spiritual; ❏ Material; ❏ Psychological;
❏ Other: _____
Did you speak about: ❏ God? ❏ Gospel? ❏ Bible study?
❏ Other? _____
Spiritual Response: ❏ Open; ❏ Closed;
❏ Other: _____
Would another contact be worthwhile? ❏ Yes; ❏ No;
❏ Other: _____
Approximate age: _____   Religious background: _____

43

WHERE TO GET FREE EVANGELISM MATERIALS AND RESOURCES

Free Word Ministries, Inc.
4 Electric Ave.
East Greenbush, NY. 12061
Telephone: (214)853-5685

"Free Word Ministries is currently receiving Gospels of John free of charge from ***Absolutely Free, Inc.*** This generous organization has supplied millions of copies of Scripture in several different languages (English, Russian, French, Dutch, Arabic) all around the world. World Missionary Press, Inc. also supplied millions of copies of scripture booklets around the world on various subjects (i.e. How to Know God, The Power of God and The Amazing Life of Jesus Christ) in over 300 languages for free".

Ministry Resource Links

Bibles, and New Testaments

(612)338-0500

Gospel of John/Tracts Free

Grace Evangelistic Ministries (541)496-3046

(615)3713929

Christian Brotherhood Newsletter 214)853-5685

(949)470-9883

800)910-4226

Child and Youth Evangelism
David C. Cook Church Ministries (800)323-7543

College Evangelism
800)743-6374

Jewish Evangelism
Friends of Israel Gospel Ministry (800)257-7843

Muslim Evangelism
Arab World Ministries(800)447-3566

Roman Catholic Evangelism
C.E.C. 502)895-5390
Proclaiming the Gospel (972)495-0485

Jails and Prison Ministries
Break Point 800)995-8777
Gospel Advocate 800)251-8446

Cult Information
Christian Research Institute 888)700-CRI1
U.M.I. Ministries(800)654-3992

Prayer Evangelism
Prayer Power 800)949-PRAY
Pray Arlington 817)300-0004
Pray Texas 915)580-4888

Follow Up Material
A Discipled Nation 517)323-6233
Bible Works 800)74-BIBLE
Countryside Bible Church 817)488-5381
Discovery Series 800)598-7221

Evangelism Training

Luis Palau Evangelistic Assoc. 800)275-5847

The Gideons International In Canada

501 Imperial Road North
Guelph, Ontario, Canada N1H 7A2

Email: info@gideons.ca
Telephone: 519.823.1140
Fax: 519.767.1913
Bibles-By-Phone: 1.888.482.4253

http://www.gideons.org.uk/BibleHelps/index.asp

Evangelical Tract Distributors

Evangelical Tract Distributors
P.O. Box 146
Edmonton, Albert
a Canada T5J 2G9
tel. 1-780-477-1538
fax. 1-780-477-3795
online comments/feedback form
www.evangelicaltract.com

Fellowship Tract League
Tracts In Many Languages. FREE!
Fellowship Tract League (FTL)
PO Box 164
Lebanon, Ohio 45036 USA
ph: 513-494-1075
ph: 513-401-1075
www.fellowshiptractleague.org

Liberty Gospel Tracts & Bible Courses

(EXCELLENT FOR NEW BELIEVERS!)
11845 West Carson City Rd., Greenville, MI USA 48838
Email: libertyb@pathwaynet.com

World Missionary Press, Inc.

P.O. Box 120 -- New Paris, IN 46553
Fax: 1-574-831-2161
"This printing ministry offers **FREE AS LORD PROVIDES** gospel printed materials for use world wide. Over 310 language available. Shipping also free. Please let them know that you are requesting KJV booklets in English as they have many available. Sure Mercies Outreach recommends KJV gospel study in Matthew, John & Psalms. Also KJV Gospel of John. KJV New Testament. Booklets in KJV called Help From Above & The Way To God. This printing ministry is excellent for larger orders"!
EMAIL World Missionary Press Here

Bible Baptist Church--James L. Melton Publications

Free Gospel printed materials for study and evangelism (donation appreciated but not required).125 E. Maple,
Sharon TN USA 38255
Go There Now! Email: MeltonLion@aol.com

Bible Way Baptist Church

FREE KING JAMES BIBLE TRACTS -- VIEW OUR TRACT GALLERY AND ORDER ON LINE..
P.O. BOX 2424, CLARKESVILLE, GA 30523
USA
Email: deneaubps@juno.com

Faithful Witness Tract Society

"If you are an independent Baptist missionary serving on a foreign field, the Faithful Witness Tract Society of Community Baptist Church in Bradenton, Florida, USA, offers free tracts, postage paid. Contact them with your tract needs at info@seekingchrist.net".

FamilyNet International Inc.

P.O. Box 451951 Garland, Texas 75045 USA
Phone:(214) 257-0229
FamilyNet provides, free of charge, Source of Light Bible Correspondence Courses via US Mail. Multiple students are welcome.
Contact them
bible.course@family-bible.us

Middletown Bible Church

349 East St.
"Middletown, CT 06457 [Phone: (860) 346-0907]
This ministry offers loads of materials available for downloading/printing off their webpage. They also offer printed materials through postal mail for a very, very low cost! Including Sunday School Materials, Doctrinal Worksheets, Bible study materials, doctrinal studies on various topics, tools for evangelism, studies for new believers & papers/booklets on modern issues". =
Contact them

Pilgrim Fundamental Baptist Press, INC.

P.O. Box 1832, Elkton,
MD USA 21922 (410) 620-2697
Email: pfbaptistpress@pfbaptistpress.org

Global Recordings Network

"GRN has centres, bases and agents in more than 30 countries. They go by a number of different names, such as Gospel Recordings, Language Recordings, Audio Gospel, Good News Media and others.
The Vision of GRN is that people might hear and understand God's word in their heart language - especially those who are oral communicators and those who do not have Scriptures in a form they can access. They do this by producing culturally appropriate audio and audio-visual materials.
Recordings are now available in 5745 different languages"!

Tracts4God

Fundamental KJB tracts using the law to point to Christ. (Download & Print)

International Tract Ministry

271 Cleveland, Trenton, MI USA 48183 (or)
1706 Old Goddard Rd. Lincoln Park, MI USA 48146
Email: rgb@gospeltracts.com

Bible Tracts, Inc.

PO Box 188 Bloomington, IL
61702-0188
Phone: (309) 828-6888
Fax: (309) 828-0573
Free Gospel Tracts
"Over the 65+ years of ministry, BTI has expanded, printing in more than 100 languages and even into Braille. The concern of our founder was that no gospel worker be in need of evangelistic tools. That remains our passion and is what has motivated us to print over 528 million tracts and give them away for free".

MASS MEDIA OUTREACH MINISTRIES

(International Missions Outreach Of Freedom Baptist Church)
MAIN OFFICE: P. O. Box 14067
Greenville, South Carolina 29610 USA

MMOM- Literature/PrintShop/Overseas Division:

P.O. Box 14892 * Greenville, SC 29610 USA
Dr. Donnie D. Whitlock: P.O. Box 14892 * Greenville,
SC 29610 USA
OR
"You can email us at: MassMedia1@juno.com /
docwhitlock@yahoo.com
We are presently sending Gospel literature and study materials to national pastors, laymen and missionaries on the field".

Bible Baptist Church

FREE 8 Lesson Bible Correspondence Course With Certificate Of Completion
3338 Main St. P.O. Box 42,
Lupton, MI USA 48635 (989) 473-3151

Russian Gospel Ministries (Main Office)

Offers many helps to Russian evangelists & Bible printing..
3128 Lexington Park Drive
P.O. Box 1188 Elkhart,
IN USA 46515 (219) 522-3486
Email: RGMI@juno.com

King James Bible Society,
527 Benjulyn Road,
Cantonment, FL 32533
(850) 968-5903
"They seek to provide KJV Bibles, New Testaments, and gospel portions for missionaries and national pastors who could not otherwise afford to purchase their own. Through quarterly projects they ship consignments of scriptures free of charge to doctrinally sound, faithful distributors. This ministry is faith based."

Burn your own Evangelism CD—(*FreeEvangelismCDs.com*).
http://tracts4free.com/free-tracts

44

How to Obtain Ministerial Credentials

Canadian Christian Ministries

Ministerial Training and Credentials

CCM School of Ministry offers three levels of minister certification courses:

- Certificate in Ministerial Studies Level One
- Certificate in Ministerial Studies Level Two
- Diploma in Ministerial Studies

Applicants for Lay Minister Credentials must complete the Certificate in Ministerial Studies Level One.

Applicants for Licensed Minister Credentials must complete the Certificate in Ministerial Studies Level Two.

Applicants for Ordained Minister Credentials must complete the Diploma in Ministerial Studies.

All are self study courses which can be done at your own time and pace. Each course has an Assignment Booklet. Students must answer the questions in the booklet and mail the completed Assignment Booklet to CCM for grading.

To receive ministerial credentials with CCM, you must complete an application form, pay the applicable fee and complete the applicable ministerial certification course. All credentials are valid for the calendar year in which they are issued and must be renewed annually on the first day of January every year.

Ministerial ID Cards

All Ministers credentialed with CCM are issued a Ministerial ID card for the purpose of identification and association with the organization. The ID card is a laminated card the same size of a business card and carries the following information:

Credential Certificates

All Ministers credentialed with CCM are also issued a Credential Certificate such as Lay Minister Certificate, Licensed Minister Certificate or Ordained Minister Certificate. There are no expiry dates for credential certificates.

Register Your Ministry

If you plan on running a ministry or church that will receive donations of tithes and offering from its members or the public, you will need to register your ministry or church as a charitable religious organization with the government of Canada. Once registered your ministry will receive a business number and will be able to operate legally in Canada and issue tax receipts.

All applicants must provide a governing document also known as a constitution. CCM can assist you with a constitution and your registration to insure compliance under the Income Tax Act. This service is provided by CCM staff for a small service fee. CCM can also assist you in filing your church/ministry annual tax returns.

Marriage License

Ontario Marriage Licenses are issued by the Office of the Registrar General, Government of Ontario. Therefore, to be eligible to receive a marriage license through CCM you must meet the following criteria; you must be:

- A Resident of Ontario.
- An Ordained Minister with CCM.
- A Pastor, Assistant Pastor, Missionary or Evangelist of a registered ministry or church located in Ontario.

Benefits of Association with CCM

When you receive ministerial credentials with CCM you will enjoy the following benefits:

1. You will become part of the CCM network of Ministers.
2. You will receive a Ministerial ID card and credentials.
3. You will be affirmed by a reputable Christian organization.
4. Your name, rank and ministry will be listed in the CCM Register of Ministers.
5. You will have access to leadership seminars and conferences organized by CCM and its associated ministries and churches.
6. You will have the opportunity to network with other ministers, ministries and churches.
7. You will have the opportunity to post your ministry/church upcoming events such as prayer breakfast, concert, and leadership seminars on the CCM website free of charge.
8. You will have access to CCM ministry services at a reduced cost.

CCM is your organization for all you need to legally operate a church or ministry in Canada. The following services are provided through the office of the General Overseer:

Free Services:
1. Marriage License for its Ordained Ministers.
2. Letters of recommendation or reference for all its Ministers.
3. Listing your church on the CCM website
4. Listing of your church's upcoming events on the CCM website.
5. Links from the CCM website to your church's website.
6. Some Leadership Seminars.

Services for a low service fee:
1. Lay Minister Certification Course.
2. Licensed Minister Certification Course.
3. Ordained Minister Certification Course.
4. Registering your church or ministry with the Government of Canada.

5. Preparing the annual Tax Return for your ministry or church for Canada Revenue Agency.
6. Some Leadership Seminars may require a small fee to cover the cost of materials.

What is CCM

Canadian Christian Ministries also known as CCM was established to oversee the training, credentialing and ongoing mentoring of Christian Ministers and Religious Workers.

CCM is a religious, non-denominational organization dedicated to the advancement of the Christian faith by providing religious instruction and a mentoring relationship with ministers and their work, for guidance, encouragement and fellowship. This relationship will provide a spiritual, moral and professional covering for ministers.

Organizational Structure

Canadian Christian Ministries is governed by a Board of Directors consisting of a General Overseer, a General Secretary, a General Treasurer and other officers. The General Overseer is the Chairman of the Board of Directors of CCM.

Mission and Vision Statement

Our mission is to provide ministerial training, credentials and affiliation for Christian workers who run their own independent ministries. These workers include, but are not limited to, Pastors, Evangelist, Missionaries, Musicians, Singers, Teachers, Worship Dancers, Writers, Producers and Compassionate Workers. Our vision is to empower Christian workers, ministries and churches for effective ministry.

Contact Information

Mailing Address
Canadian Christian Ministries
20 Coxworth Crescent
Scarborough Ontario M1B 1E3
Tel No: (416) 332 8884
Website: www.cacministries.webs.com
Email: cacministries@gmail.com

45

Funding Resources for Non-profit Organizations

Enterprising Non-Profits (enp)

EMP is a funding program that provides matching grants to nonprofit organizations in BC who are interested in starting or expanding a business. ENP program funding enables organizations to conduct planning activities related to the development of a business venture.

   Contact Information

David LePage, Program Manager
Telephone: 604-871-5477
Fax: 604-709-6909
Twitter: @enp_David
Email: david@enterprisingnonprofits.ca

Alcan Inc.

Through its community investment program, Alcan contributes to Canadian nonprofits and charities in the areas of youth, education, technology,

Contact us

Rio Tinto Alcan, Head office

1188, Sherbrooke Street West
Montreal, Quebec
H3A 3G2
Canada

Telephone:
+ 1 514 848 8000

Rio Tinto Alcan, Australia

ACN 004 502 694
Level 2, 443 Queen Street
Brisbane, Queensland 4000
Australia

Telephone:
+61 7 3867 1711

+61 7 3218 3555

Fax:

FedEx Canada (National: Mississauga, ON)

"FedEx is especially interested in supporting nonprofit organizations that request: 5% or less of a total project budget; contingency grants; or seed monies with the thought that other sources will contribute matching amounts. Charitable shipping is limited to emergency, disaster or life-threatening situations coordinated through a nonprofit organization, disaster relief agency, or agency of the federal, provincial, or local government."

Mailing Address for All Requests

FedEx Canada Community Relations
5985 Explorer Drive
Mississauga, Ontario
L4W 5K6

Hbc Foundation

Each year the Hbc Foundation, by working closely with local and national organizations across the country, invests more than $10 million towards three key areas: building healthy families, building strong communities, and inspiring Canadians.

General Inquiries

- P.O. Box 223
- Station A
- Scarborough, Ontario
- M1K 5C1

- Canada
- Telephone toll free in Canada
- 1-866-746-7422
- Monday to Friday
- 9:00am - 5:00pm local time

Loblaw

"Loblaw provides a number of forms of community investment, including administering the President's Choice Children's Charity Foundation. They also offer local store donations and grants, an after school program grant, and a colleague volunteer grant program. The company's granting priorities include healthy kids, green communities, and the support of local food banks. They also support religious organizations."

Grant request can only be done by email at giving@loblaw.ca.

Manulife Financial

"By promoting healthy futures, supporting leaders of tomorrow and by being a partner in the community, globally, Manulife Financial is committed to giving back to the community. They offer funding to many different countries; funding is done online however, you can contact the below information for information."

E-mail
webmaster@manulife.com

Phone
(416) 852-6983

Fax
(416) 926-5410

Mail
Karen Bannister
Manulife Financial
200 Bloor St. E.
Toronto, Ontario
M4W 1E5

Maple Leaf Foods

"Philanthropic giving focuses on three sectors: effective health research and services; community and social services programs; and education, particularly in the area of food nutrition research."

between 8:30 - 5:30 EST
1-800-268-3708
LETTER Maple Leaf Foods Consumer Affairs
P.O. Box 55021
Montréal, Quebec, H3G 2W5

Microsoft Canada

"Microsoft Canada believes it has a responsibility to help bridge the digital divide. Through its I Can Community Programs, Microsoft assists charities, nonprofits, and community groups across the country with support through financial aid, software, services, and volunteer support by its employees."
http://www.microsoft.com/canada/media/default.aspx

Syncrude Community Investment Program

"The community program focuses on the areas of education, environment, health and safety, science and technology, Aboriginal relations, local community development, arts and culture, and recreation. Their Good Neighbours program supports the efforts of employees by providing grants to the groups for which they volunteer."

Community Investment Program

Maggie Grant

Community Investment Advisor

780-790-6356

Postal Address

Head Office
PO Bag 4023, Fort McMurray
Alberta Canada T9H 3H5

Team Up Foundation (Regional: Toronto, ON)

"Run by Maple Leaf Sports & Entertainment, this is the official foundation of four local sports teams, including the Toronto Maple Leafs and the Toronto Raptors. The foundation funds projects focusing on at-risk youth in Ontario, including projects that involve hockey, basketball, soccer, or other physical education initiatives, as well as community and social services programs."

http://www.mlseteamupfoundation.org/home

Whole Foods Market (National)

"Each Whole Foods store is responsible for community giving within their local area. Not only does each store provide food to local food banks and shelters, but they also hold several "5%" days throughout the year, where 5% of the sales of that day are donated to local groups. Donation request forms are available from each individual store."

http://www.wholefoodsmarket.com/values/giving.php

Government Funding Programs

British Columbia Gaming Grants (British Columbia)

"Government gaming grants allow eligible organizations to apply for gaming revenues to support a broad range of programs and services."

Web site:http://www.pssg.gov.bc.ca/gaming/grants/index.htm

Canada Mortgage and Housing Corporation - Shelter Enhancement Program (National)

Canada Mortgage and Housing Corporation (CMHC) offers financial assistance to assist in the repair, rehabilitation and improvement of existing shelters and assists in the acquisition or construction of new shelters and second-stage housing for victims of family violence.

Contact Us

To find out how to apply for financial assistance or for more information about these programs please call CMHC toll free at **1-800-668-2642**

Community Initiatives Program (CIP) (Alberta)

"Provides funds to enhance and enrich project-based initiatives throughout Alberta. CIP supports project-based initiatives in areas such as community services, seniors' services, libraries, arts and culture, sports, education, health and recreation."

Community Spirit Program
Alberta Culture and Community Spirit
9th Floor, Standard Life Building
10405 Jasper Avenue
Edmonton, AB T5J 4R7
community.spirit@gov.ab.ca
780-644-8604
To call toll-free in Alberta dial 310-0000.

Community Initiatives Program
Culture and Community Spirit
Suite 212, 17205 - 106A Avenue
Edmonton, Alberta T5S 1M7

Or

Community Facility Enhancement Program
Culture and Community Spirit
Suite 212, 17205 - 106A Avenue
Edmonton, Alberta T5S 1M7

780-422-9598
Toll free at 1-800-642-3855 Main Line (780) 427-0387

FedNor (Regional)

"FedNor is a federal regional development organization that is committed to helping traditionally under-represented populations participate more fully in the economic development of Northern Ontario. Resources and funding are available to help create an environment in which communities can thrive and people can prosper."

Online: info@ic.gc.ca
Telephone: 613-954-5031
Toll-free: 1-800-328-6189 (Canada)

TTY (for hearing-impaired only): 1-866-694-8389 (toll-free)
Fax: 613-954-2340

Business hours are 8:30 a.m. to 5:00 p.m. (Eastern Time), Monday to Friday.

Mailing Address:
Industry Canada Web Service Centre
Industry Canada
C.D. Howe Building
235 Queen Street
Ottawa, Ontario K1A 0H5

New Horizons for Seniors (National)

"Through Social Development Canada, this program provides funding for community-based projects across the country that encourage seniors to continue to play an important role in their community. Calls for applications are issued once or twice a year."

New Horizons for Seniors Program
Human Resources and Skills Development Canada
333 North River Road, 2A
Ottawa, Ontario K1A 0L1

Toll free:
1 800 277-9914

Teletypewriter:
1 800 255-4786

Nunavut Department of Culture, Language, Elders and Youth (Regional)

"Provides funding in the form of grants and contributions to community-based, non-profit organizations and individuals. This funding is set aside to assist those who have an idea or project that contributes to the preservation and/or promotion of Nunavut's culture, heritage, language or amateur sport."

For assistance with grant and contribution applications:
Toll Free: 1-866-934-2035

Our Address is:
Department of Culture, Language, Elders and Youth
Box 1000, Stn, 800
Iqaluit, Nunavut
X0A 0H0

Status of Women Canada (National)

"Status of Women Canada (SWC) is a federal government organization that promotes the full participation of women in the economic, social and democratic life of Canada. They provide funding for women's programs, with an emphasis on economic security and prosperity, leadership, as well as community programs that encourage women to participate in their communities."

National

Status of Women Canada
123 Slater Street
10th Floor
Ottawa, ON
K1P 1H9
Toll free: 1-866-902-2719
Local: 613-995-7835
Fax: 613-947-0761
infonational@swc-cfc.gc.ca

Atlantic

Status of Women Canada
33 Weldon Street, Unit 230
Moncton, NB
E1C 0N5
Toll free: 1-877-851-3644
Local: 506-851-3644
Fax: 506-851-3610
infoatlantic@swc-cfc.gc.ca

Quebec and Nunavut

Status of Women Canada
1564 St. Denis Street
Montréal, QC
H2X 3K2
Toll free: 1-888-645-4141
Local: 514-283-3150
Fax: 514-283-3449
infoquebec-nunavut@swc-cfc.gc.ca

Ontario

Status of Women Canada
123 Slater Street
10th Floor
Ottawa, ON
K1P 1H9
Toll free: 1-866-599-7259
Local: 613-995-3995
Fax: 613-947-0761
infoontario@swc-cfc.gc.ca

West, Northwest Territories and Yukon

Status of Women Canada
Suite 1001, Highfield Place
10010 - 106 Street NW
Edmonton, AB
T5J 3L8
Toll free: 1-866-966-3640
Local: 780-495-3839
Fax: 780-495-2315
Toll free fax: 1-866-967-3640
infowest@swc-cfc.gc.ca

Youth Justice Renewal Initiative (National)

"Administered by the Department of Justice, funding through this program is directed to organizations and programs addressing youth justice. There are three areas of funding available - the main fund, the anti-drug component, and the guns, drugs, and gangs priority." http://www.justice.gc.ca/eng/pi/yj-jj/fund-fond/fund-fond.html

Department of Justice Canada
284 Wellington Street
Ottawa, Ontario
Canada K1A 0H8

General Inquiries
Communications Branch
(613) 957-4222
TDD/TTY: (613) 992-4556

Microcredit Funding Programs

Alterna Savings

(National) Alterna Savings Community Micro Loan program provides business loans along with a full range of financial services to self-employed individuals who would not otherwise qualify or have access to credit from other financial institutions. **http://www.alterna.ca**

VanCity (British Columbia)

Innovative loan products include the Peer Lending Program, a unique group lending method for securing small scale credit, and Self Reliance Loans for individuals requiring larger credit for start up or expansion. Web site:https://www.vancity.com

Financial Help for Single Mothers

Contains information on more than 30 financial grants and assistance for single moms including college aid, housing subsidies, food stamp benefits, childcare insurance, and more. Website: http://www.financialhelpsinglemother.com

International Information Sources

Directory of Development Organizations, a guide to international organizations, governments, private sector institutions, development agencies, grantmakers, banks, microfinance institutions, and development consulting firms. Website: http://www.devdir.org. Email info@devdir.org

Funders Online, a searchable directory of European and American foundations maintained by the European Foundation. web site: **http://www.fundersonline.org**

Most information compiled from: http://www.charityvillage.com/cv/ires/fund.asp

46

OBTAINING CHARITY NUMBER

Charity Number can be obtained from the Canada Revenue
Starting a Nonprofit or Charity
Last updated March 2010 **CharityVillage.com**

Initial Questions

The nonprofit sector is one of the fastest growing sectors in North America right now, and with almost 150,000 registered charities and nonprofits currently operating in Canada, it shows no signs of slowing down. Of course, as more and more organizations are added to the mix, groups must become increasingly creative in the planning and carrying out of their mission. Keeping this in mind, there are several questions that should be considered before you begin the process of starting your own nonprofit organization or charity.

- Do you have a clear understanding of the problem or need you want to address? Is that need ongoing or short-term?
- Are there other similar organizations currently operating that already address this need? If so, will you be competing with these groups for funds, resources, or clients?
- Do other individuals agree that such an organization is needed? Are they willing to volunteer their time and energy to help get things started?
- Will you be able to locate the resources and finances necessary to achieve your mission?
- Do you understand the rules, regulations, and requirements of running a nonprofit organization or charity in your region?

Planning

Once you've decided to go ahead with your organization, there are a few initial steps that should be taken.

- Assemble a group of like-mined individuals who believe in the cause and are willing to dedicate themselves to its initial undertaking. These founding members will likely form the organization's first board of directors. Under provincial legislation by which nonprofit societies are registered, a board of directors is a legal requirement. It is also required by the federal government if you plan to apply for charitable status.

- Discuss and clarify the issues or needs that the organization will address and what your next steps will be.

- Agree upon and write a mission statement to describe what your group aims to achieve.

- Choose a name for the organization and figure out important logistics, such as where the organization will be housed, how it will be financed, what role each person will play, and what their responsibilities will be.

- Decide whether to incorporate your organization, become a registered charity, or both.

Incorporation

You can incorporate your organization either provincially or federally and the process is much the same as it is for incorporating a company. It is relatively straight forward, and can be handled by a competent solicitor with some experience in this area. Without incorporating or registering, your organization will not be legally recognized as a nonprofit, nor will your group's name be protected against use by other legal entities. Below are links to government web pages that deal specifically with nonprofit incorporation.

- <u>Canada</u>
  - <u>Not-for-Profit Corporations Act</u>

- Income Tax Guide to the Non-Profit Organization (NPO) Information Return
- T1044 Non-Profit Organization (NPO) Information Return

Charitable Status

The Canada Revenue Agency (CRA) -- formerly Revenue Canada -- is the government department responsible for granting organizations charitable tax status. The process routinely takes 6 months to 18 months and requires applicants to fulfill a number of requirements. One of the major advantages of obtaining charitable status, is that the organization is able to issue receipts to donors for income tax purposes. This can be a major advantage when soliciting for donations. In addition, charities receive certain tax exemptions.

Not to be overlooked however, is the fact that registered charities are subject to a number of regulations and restrictions. One such restriction is the limitation on a charity's ability to advocate for a specific cause. Currently, groups with charitable tax status can only use 10% of their budget for advocacy. As well, charities are required to file an income tax return at least every two years and these files are available to the public, along with other official documents pertaining to the organization. Below are relevant links to the CRA web site:

Canada Revenue Agency now makes the following information publicly available about registered charities:

- a charity's governing documents (i.e., the letters patent, articles of incorporation, trust deed, constitution);
- the application form (completed by a charity when it sought registration or re-registration);
- the notification of registration or re-registration (a letter sent by the Department to notify a charity of its registered status);
- the letter the Department sends to a charity that has been de-registered, explaining the reasons for
- the Department's action; and
- the names of the persons who are or have been directors/trustees of the charity, and the periods during which they served as directors/trustees.

To request public information on charities, **call 1-800-267-2384** for toll free long distance calls.

Helpful Organizations

- **VolunteerBC**

    Offers a comprehensive resource tool designed to help groups through the various stages of organizational planning.

- **Volunteer Lawyers Service**

    The Volunteer Lawyers Service provides free legal assistance to nonprofit and charitable organizations in Ontario, including a broad range of business law services: employment law; duties and liabilities of directors; real estate and leases; trademark registration; privacy; contracts; etc.

How to Get a Charity Tax ID Number
By an eHow Contributor

In order for your charity or non-profit organization to buy goods tax-exempt, accept donations and provide proof of tax deductions or even open a bank account, you will need a charity tax ID number. Follow these simple steps to get a charity tax ID number.

Difficulty: Moderately Challenging
Instructions

1. Obtain Form SS-4 from the Internal Revenue Service. This is an application for an employer identification number, which is the same as tax ID number according the IRS. You can download the form directly from the IRS website.

2. Complete Form SS-4 according the attached instructions. You will need to read all the instructions carefully since there will be some sections that may or may not apply to your charity.

3. Submit Form SS-4 in a variety of ways. You can complete and submit the form online in one easy step, download and print the

form and send to the address indicated on the form or submit it via phone or fax.

4. Wait for the IRS to issue your charity tax ID number or employer identification number. The quickest way to get your tax ID number is by applying online. A faxed application will take about a week for a response, and a mailed Form SS-4 should take 4 to 6 weeks to

Read more: How to Get a Charity Tax ID Number | eHow.com http://www.ehow.com/how_2272979_get-charity-tax-id-number.html#ixzz1EM3sv0K5

47

MISSION OPPORTUNITIES—LINKS

Short Term Mission—Canadian Baptist Ministries
www.cbmin.org/cbm/

Short Term Missions Opportunities—Youth group projects, summer outreaches.
www.missionfinder.org

Short Term Missions Directory
http://www.missionsfestvancouver.ca/opportunities.cfm

Be a Missionay in Australia—Missionary Training in Australia
http://ywamrto.org

Evangelism Training Opportunity

Evangelism God's Way provides

Free Evangelism Training

Every Saturday from 11:00am to 1:30pm

Location: Canada Christian College

50 Gervais Drive, Don Mills On. 5th floor. Telephone:416-526-0763

Special Acknowledgements:

Pastor Dr. Rondo Thomas

Dr Roy Sommerville

Minister Wilkie Colquhoun

Evangelist Nick Parisi

Evangelist Audrey/ Elmer Cachnela

Minister Yvonne Harvot

Pastor Alimay/ Falcon Campbell

Evangelist Charlie/ Teena Chandrapal

Pastor Naomi Lewis

Evangelist Elvie Bangit

Minister Moreen Hosannah

Andre Colquhoun

Jackie Crawford

Sister Polina Timal

Marites Celestial

Minister Josie Signorelli

Evangelist Grace John

Evangelist Shaw

Dolly Mapanao

Minister Barbara Bacic-Leones

Chris Clay

Cindee Crowley

BIBLIOGRAPHY

1. The Nelson Study Bible, New King James Version. Copyright 1997 by Thomas Neilson, Inc. Printed in USA 1997.
2. George W. Knight and Rayburn W. Ray. The Illustrated Bible Dictionary. Published by Barbour Publishing, Inc. Ohio. 2005.
3. Henrietta C. Mears, What the Bible is all About, Published by Regal Books, Venture, Califonia, USA. interference. Printed in USA. Copyright 1997..
4. Ron Rhodes. Understanding the Bible From A-Z. Published by Harvest House Publishers. Eugene, Oregon 2003.
5. Frank Charles Thompson, D.D. Ph.D. The Thompson Chain-Reference Bible, KJV. Indiana U.S.A: Copyright 1988. The B. B. Kirkbridge Bible Company, Inc. entered at Stationer's Hall London, 2000.
6. Dr. Miles Munroe, Understand the purpose and power of Prayer, Copyright 2002 by Dr. Myles Maunroe. Library of Congress Cataloging-in-Publication Data. Printed in USA.
7. Elmer L. Towns, Concise Bible Doctrine Copyright 1983, 2006 by Elmer L. Tower, Published by AMG Publishers. Printed in the USA.
8. Johan D. Tangelder, www.reformedreflections.ca, April, 1972
9. D. James Kennedy, Evangelism Explosion, Wheaton, IL, Tyndale House Publishers, 1977, p6
10. @ Spotlight Ministries, Vincent McCann, 2002, spotlightministries.org.uk
11. Thomas Rainer, Effective Evangelistic Churches, Nashville, TN, 1996, p.19, 20, 41

12. Ralph D. Winter & Steven C. Hawthorne, Patrick Johnstone, Prespectives on the World Christian Movement, Forth Edition Published 2009, USA.

13. Crusaders Raise Profile, Tampa Tribune, October 17, 1998

14. Henrietta C. Mears, Foreword by Billy Graham. What the Bible Is All About. Published by Regal Books, Venture, California, U.S.A. 1990. Copyright 1997. page 496

15. D. James Kennedy, Evangelism Explosion, Wheaton, IL, Tyndale House Publishers, 1977, p.6

16. christianministriesintl.org/articles/15.html

CPSIA information can be obtained at www.ICGtesting.com
234164LV00001B/15/P

9 781449 718121